VENICE CARNIVAL

PHOTOGRAPHY BY VIRGINIO FAVALE • ESSAY BY PAOLO ALEI

ARTMEDIAPRESS

Acknowledgments

In this visual and verbal account of the Venice Carnival we have depended greatly on the artistic genius of all Venetian citizens and visitors who express their tribute to the Serenissima with spectacular costumes and masks in the elegant public spaces of Piazza San Marco and in the privacy of the Grand Canal palaces. Many of the Venice Carnival protagonists have been available for photography and interview: the Don Francesco family, Pier Paolo and French friends Marie Laure, Frederick and Yanick; Monica Alei, Igino Giacchetti, Magda and Margot Groja, Caterina and Costanza Hreglich and, finally, the two major protagonists of the Venice Carnival, Count Emile Targhetta and maestro Giorgio Arvati, who went beyond the realms of kindness in posing for our photos. We have depended greatly on the generosity of the directors and staff of Caffè Florian, Caffè Quadri and the Danieli and Luna Hotels, who allowed access to their magnificent salons at a busy time. We owe an incalculable debt to Signora Giovanna Barbiero and her International Association for the Carnival of Venice, who invited our team to Ca' Zanardi for the Mardi Gras party, and the organisation of the Ballo del Doge at Palazzo Pisani Moretta, which was organised by Signora Antonia Sautter and Prince Maurice Agosti. A great thank you goes to all those chroniclers, historians, poets, painters and photographers who have written and depicted the Venice Carnival before us, especially Adrian Giurgea and Danilo Reato who have magisterially studied the concept of Carnival and its significance in Venice, providing inspiration for many future writers on the subject. We are grateful to *Sunday Times* journalist Peter Martin for his helpful suggestions, and the director of the Maria Callas Association, Bruno Tosi, for his kind assistance. Finally, to two special people who have contributed more than anybody else to our project: Max Elijah Grossman and Toshiko Tozawa. Max's suggestions on the text have been invaluable. Toshiko has assisted each stage of the photographic process but above all has worked in a spirit of cooperation that has ushered in moments of mutual esteem, genuine friendship and great enthusiasm. This book is dedicated to all those who believe in and have stimulated this project, above all Venice itself which, with its magic beauty, has inspired every moment of our work.

The Publisher

I am deeply indebted to Max Elijah Grossman, an excellent scholar and special friend who kindly offered his critical attention as reader of my work. I am grateful to Aikaterini Psoma, whose warm heart and affection made my days of research in London a memorable experience. I especially value the contribution of my parents (Manlio and Erminia Alei) for having introduced me to the Carnival of Venice when I was a child.

Paolo Alei

Published in Great Britain in 2003 by ARTMEDIA PRESS
Culvert House, Culvert Road, London SW11 5AP

ISBN: 1 902889 01 0

Printed and bound in Italy

CONTENTS

Introduction

Once did She hold the gorgeous east in fee;
And was the safeguard of the west; the worth
Of Venice did not fall below her birth,
Venice, the eldest child of liberty.
She was a maiden City, bright and free;
No guile seduced, no force could violate;
And, when she took unto herself a Mate,
She must espouse the everlasting Sea.
And what if she had seen those glories fade,
Those titles vanish, and that strength decay;
Yet shall some tribute of regret be paid
When her long life hath reached its final day:
Men are we, and must grieve when even the Shade
Of that which once was great is passed away.

(William Wordsworth, 'On the Extinction of the
Venetian Republic')

Carnival is a time of transition in both the ecclesiastical and astral calendars. It is an interval of mysterious days and nights between Christmas and Lent when the equinox leads nature from darkness to light. Ancient beliefs suggest that in February, when Mother Earth is a deserted land awaiting resurrection, the dead leave the underworld to participate in the business of the living. With various types of instruments, human beings make rustic noises that exhort nature to regenerate, and camouflage themselves with disguises in order to participate in the rituals of the soul. This exchange between humanity and nature, life and death, is embodied in the mask, a mysterious object that paradoxically evokes death with laughter. Imbued with a kind of enigmatic licence, the mask projects a different identity, empowering its wearer with a new authority while hypnotising observers with fear and curiosity. Through this magical device people may abandon their inhibitions, reverse their social roles, alter their personalities and even choose their sexuality. Why did Venice become the major European proponent for such revelry?

Venice is a city that has often been imagined and represented as a personification, an allegory, a theatre of death, a chimerical place. The humanist poet Petrarch called Venice 'mundus alter' (another world), highlighting the uniqueness of Venetian civilisation.[1] Between the fourteenth and eighteenth centuries Venice often inspired hyperbole and in the minds of its artists and citizens was contemporaneously personified as the Virgin Mary, Venus, Dea Roma and Justice. Painters vied to depict the city as a beautiful woman robed in oriental brocades, adorned with precious jewels, crowned by angels and praised by the gods. From the Middle Ages allegory was her mask and spectacle her costume.

With six months of official Carnival every year, rich and poor alike lived in a Utopian world where city and citizens exhibited their masks. The festival reached its climax around 1500 during the Renaissance, entered a phase of poetic decadence in the eighteenth century (the Settecento), and came to its conclusion at the dawn of the nineteenth century. The finale occurred when Napoleon's troops invaded the Veneto in 1797. With this shocking irruption, Venice suddenly saw its glorious past and personified myth vanish, while its traditions and freedom disintegrated.

In the aftermath of the decline poets described the Lagoon as a lugubrious space where gondolas seemed like black coffins floating on gloomy canals. To these writers the sound of water lapping against Byzantine and Renaissance marbles no longer suggested dominion

and prosperity but whispered a frightening tale of imminent demise. For Venetians in the nineteenth century Carnival was a mere reflection of what it had represented during the Renaissance, and feasts survived only as vague memories, acted out in the privacy of theatres and palaces, until their abolition by the twentieth-century Fascist regime.

In 1980, almost two hundred years after the Napoleonic invasion, the Venetians revived their Carnival, seemingly as a reaction against fear and hysteria in the wake of the terrorist campaign launched by the Red Brigade at the end of the 1960s. The revival was spontaneous, as if the city – considered soulless by many – had suddenly exploded with frenzied joy. Between 1979 and 1980 Maurizio Scaparro, a theatre director, and Paolo Portoghesi, an architect, were experimenting with theatre in the already ephemeral spaces of the city. One night an unexpected event surprised the two men: in the dark hours before Ash Wednesday, Venice was suddenly invaded by thousands of people. A gigantic crowd wearing masks exploded in a dance of liberation under the spectre of a golden basilica and the silhouette of a Gothic palace in one of the most beautiful public squares in the world: Piazza San Marco. Meanwhile the palaces of the Grand Canal, their lights reflected on water and marble, hosted banquets inspired by folly, megalomania and hedonism. The lethargic Venetian winter of 1980 was animated by a Babylonian 'happening'. On that legendary night the Venice Carnival, a new symbol of freedom and *joie de vivre*, was reborn.

Gondolas waiting to take revellers
to the palaces of the Grand Canal

The text of this book will trace the history of the Venice Carnival through a study of media, customs, objects and documents: from paintings and poems to decrees and laws, from the theatre on stage to the theatre of life, from feasts and chronicles to masks and costumes, from the sound of water to the music of Vivaldi. The text flows alongside the extraordinary photographs of Virginio Favale, who presents and explores the Carnival of today. His visual documents bear witness to the last remaining masque of the twentieth century in all its private decadence. In addition to their artistic and aesthetic value, Virginio's images communicate a certain malaise symptomatic of the last *fin de siècle*. His work investigates a romantic spleen in the age of technology by penetrating the forms and emotions of the masks of Piazza San Marco.

Notes
1 P. Fortini Brown, *The Renaissance in Venice* (London, 1997), p. 9.

Origins

Festive feathers, lace and jewels

Like nature, society reveals nothing, certainly not its deepest secrets, without ceremonies.[1]

Carnival is one of the oldest feasts surviving into the third millennium. Its origins are as ancient as civilisation itself. In ancient Babylon there was an inscription indicating that at a certain time of year masters and slaves reversed their roles as if in a kind of transgressive game.[2] There is reason to believe that this social exchange was part of a celebration that occurred during springtime when the equinox marked the beginning of the Assyrian year. In Mesopotamia, as in most ancient civilisations, New Year's Eve coincided with the equinox and symbolised the cyclic renewal of universal laws. This transitional yet eternal phenomenon was celebrated by a religious procession that symbolically transported a god to Babylon, from heaven to earth. The Assyrians also practised several aspects of what is now known as Carnival.

Similar rituals occurred in the better-documented Dionysian revelries of ancient Greece, known by the Romans as Bacchanalia. These rituals consisted of the adoration of Dionysius–Bacchus, god of wine and licentiousness. The ancients celebrated the more grotesque and macabre aspects of culture in their evocation of gods and spirits, satyrs and bacchantes, with sounds and sacrifices. In ancient Rome sacrifices were offered in honour of Saturn and were among the most bizarre days of the Roman calendar: the Saturnalia.

The Saturnalia have often been identified as the origin of medieval Carnival, but there is still much disagreement.[3] During the ancient Roman feast, held in mid-December, homage was paid to Saturn, represented as a satyr-like king in the form of a puppet symbolically killed at the end of the ritual. Petronius' *Satyricon*, brilliantly interpreted cinematically by Federico Fellini, analyses the grotesque spirit of Roman society: the house of a Roman lord hosts an extravagant banquet celebrating debauchery in a carnivalesque style with music, dance, food, sex and laughter. Was the Saturnalia the precursor of Carnival? In spite of many similarities, Saturnalia took place in December, two months before Carnival. Moreover, the Roman festival, which occurred mainly in the familial household, had a more private character in contrast to the public Carnival, which took place in the streets and squares.

The Liberalia, another pagan feast, seems to be a more logical source. This was a rustic celebration taking place in February–March and seen as announcing the arrival of spring and celebrating the renewal of the soil. Other ceremonies from the ancient world offer further possible precedents for Carnival, making the task of retracing its origins an arduous, if not impossible enterprise.

The anthropological aspects of ancient festivals known as Lupercalia, Palilia, Consulia, Opiconsiva, Opalia, Vinalia and Genialia, formed the basis for many future components of the medieval festival. One should bear in mind that medieval Carnival, although pagan in spirit, was generally a religious event understood as an act of indulgence between the two sacred times of Christmas and Lent.[4] This type of festival was not so much an official rite as a transgressive spirit which, in different forms (Celtic or Greek), pervaded almost all European communities and civilisations north and south of the Alps, among the forests of Germany as well as along the coasts of Sicily.

Another controversial aspect of Carnival is its ambiguous etymology. The term may derive from the Latin *carne levar* or *carnelevarium*, which refers to the act of abstaining from eating meat. This is practised during Lent, the period immediately following Shrove Tuesday, the last day of Carnival, when gluttony is suppressed and fish is eaten instead of red meat. But the word *carne* means also corporeal flesh, with all its implications of plea-sure, lust and sin, which during Carnival are celebrated in language, costume and action. A further etymological source may be the words *carro naval*, a vehicle used since the earliest times for transporting the mythical King of Anarchy from one symbolic place to another. Although the relation between the meaning of Carnival and anarchy might be more a proposition than a truth, it sheds light on the very spirit of Carnival.

Anarchy embraces, probably better than any other concept, the very spirit of the festi-val in question. During the celebrations of the Middle Ages people reacted with sexual and gastronomic excess against the oppressive, strict and often miserable conditions of every-day life. Carnival therefore came to represent the negation of order at a time when politics and religion dominated both the public and private worlds. This historical aspect of medieval culture in relation to its celebrations is explored by Michail Bachtin in his fasci-nating book *Rabelais and his World*, a text that, better than any other, analyses Carnival as a spirit of irreverence, different from official culture.

In 1965 when Bachtin's seminal work was translated from Russian into English, scholars, especially semioticians, began exploring the idea of Carnival using new analytical methods. They abandoned the study of origins and etymology and concentrated on the nature of the

The myth of pictorial invention:
Casanova casting a shadow and
kissing his own image

festival itself. In his study of Rabelais, Bachtin focuses on the folk and humorous aspects of medieval and Renaissance European February feasts. He notices that irreverence and laughter permeated the role reversal that accompanied the rejection of authority and religion. According to Bachtin:

> Carnival is not a spectacle seen by the people; they live in it, and everyone participates because its very idea embraces all the people. While Carnival lasts there is no other Carnival outside it. During Carnival time life is subject only to its laws, that is, the laws of its freedom. It has a universal spirit; it is a special condition of the entire world, of the world's revival and renewal in which all take part. Such is the essence of Carnival, vividly felt by all its participants.[5]

In addition to his political theories, Bachtin's principal contribution lies in his attention to the human body and its biological functioning: eating, drinking, defecating and love-making. He highlights the body's physical peculiarities, its fatty regions, its protuberances, its excretions . . . Finally, a scholar had challenged the traditional aesthetically motivated view of the human body, exploring its vulgar, biological attributes, which are indeed emphasised during Carnival.

Although Bachtin's theories are indispensable for any analysis of popular and folkloristic festivity, they do not include a specific study of the Venice Carnival. One can assume that the latter was not an appropriate vehicle for expressing the scholar's ideas. It is true that the Venetian Carnival retained the propitiatory character of New Year's Eve: it was a time of over-indulgence before Lent and as such was a joyful feast filled with laughter, impiety and freedom. Nevertheless, it was strongly controlled by the Republic, which exploited the festival for ideological purposes. In the Lagoon, spontaneity and mirth went hand-in-hand with state-sponsored celebrations of the city's glory and its 'ideal' government, a peculiar combination of oligarchy, monarchy and democracy. The Republic played a major role in the organisation of spectacles where the lower and middle classes were often actors and protagonists together with the nobles. The social world of Carnival was under surveillance so that anarchy, especially in the Renaissance, was never a Venetian prerogative.[6] In Venice masquerades were dominated by games of incognito and did not inherently reverse social roles. Hierarchical differences were accentuated, especially in the fifteenth century; patricians exhibited their wealth with elaborate and expensive costumes. Such opulence was

For spirits, freed from mortal laws, with ease
Assume what sexes and what shape they please.
What guards the purity of melting maids,
In courtly balls and midnight masquerades.

(Alexander Pope, 'The Rape of the Lock')

So I'm coming clean, Cupid: here I am, your latest victim
Hands raised in surrender. Do what you like with me.

(Ovid, *The Erotic Poems*)

Eighteenth-century atmosphere in
the splendour of a Venetian palazzo

out of the reach of the lower classes but the wealthier merchants competed with the nobles in their choice of precious materials and jewels, until the Republic prohibited excessive display in a series of decrees. The government sought to maintain decorum in the eyes of citizens and foreigners; the *ordene antiguo* (traditional order) dominated any kind of feast or parade. The meddling of the Venetian state added a special dimension to the revelry, which otherwise would have been dominated by anarchy.

For the Republic Carnival was a flexible instrument of political propaganda, which gave vent to Venetian pride, amazed important visitors and amused the citizenry. As a welcoming ceremony and political instrument Carnival with its consequent masquerades and decoration of the entire city could be invoked and declared at any moment apart from during religious festivals. It was not just the citizens who wore masks, the city itself celebrated, even more emphatically than in other months of the year, its own myth and glory.

Notes

1 D. Gilmore, *Carnival and Culture: Sex, Symbol, and Status in Spain* (New Haven and London, 1998), p. 1.

2 D. Zamburlin, 'Il Rovesciamento dei Ruoli dalla Babilonia del 3000 A.C.', in *Guida al Carnevale di Venezia: luci di Venezia luci d'Oriente* (Venice, 1986), p. 32.

3 For more information about the archaic and non-archaic character of Carnival see, G.B. Bronzini, 'L'arcaicità del Carnevale, un Falso Antropologico', *Il Carnevale: dalla Tradizione Arcaica alla Traduzione colta del Rinascimento*, ed. M. Chiabo, F. Doglio, (Rome, 1989), pp. 69–85; and in the same publication, G. Brugnoli, 'Archetipi e no del Carnevale', pp. 41–67.

4 For a religious study of Carnival see, C. Gaignebet, *Le Carneval* (Paris, 1979).

5 M. Bachtin, *Rabelais and His World* (Indiana University Press, 1984), p. 7.

6 For an interesting investigation of upper- and lower-class history, condition, and interrelation with the nobles see, B. Pullan, *Rich and Poor in Renaissance Venice: The Social Institutions of a Catholic State, 1580 to 1620* (Cambridge, 1971).

As my eyes opened involuntarily I saw his strong hand grasp the slender neck of the fair woman and with giant's power draw it back, the blue eyes transformed with fury, the white teeth champing with rage, and the fair cheeks blazing red with passion.

(Bram Stoker, *Dracula*)

What dire offence from amorous causes springs
What mighty contests rise from trivial things.

(Alexander Pope, 'The Rape of the Lock')

An Allegorical Feast in a Personified City

Since the Middle Ages Venice had been associated with various symbolic Christian and pagan figures.[1] The town was founded in late antiquity, on the 25 March 421, the date when Christians recall the Annunciation to the Virgin. Every 25 March Venetians celebrated the meeting between Gabriel and Mary, the foundation of the city, and the first day of the calendar, in a propitiatory feast of protection and thanksgiving. Venice, like the Madonna, had so far retained her purity. In fact the Lagoon, until the arrival of Napoleon's soldiers in 1797, had never been violated by any foreign troops. Foreigners had always been welcomed as friendly visitors and wars had taken place on the mainland or on distant seas. Geographical position and divine favour assured the virginity of Venice, a unique city without fortifications, exposed and yet protected by the waters of the Mediterranean. Painters and poets developed an iconographical programme (*Venetia Figurata*) in which the city was represented as a beautiful woman in a magical space between the sea and heaven.

The concept of *Venetia Figurata* incorporated layers of Christian as well as mythological meaning.[2] Venice was often invoked as a Venus Anadyomene, for like the goddess of beauty she had arisen from the sea. A further legend compared Venice to the myth of Orpheus, who civilised wild communities, spreading culture and peace. These allusions imbued the sacred foundation of the city with ancient myth and symbolically linked the Lagoon to the classical world. The sacred and secular connotations of this complex iconographical programme became politically charged from the sixteenth century, for citizens of the Republic believed, more emphatically than before, that they were the heirs of both Troy and Rome.

The comparison between Venice and Rome is a legacy about heritage and continuity. A series of events inaugurated in the sixteenth century by Doge Andrea Gritti changed the course of history, culture and the arts. With the fall of Byzantium–Constantinople in 1457, Venice became a refuge for many Christians, who renamed the city New Byzantium. Yet, because of the Turkish expansion to the west and the consequent loss of Greek colonies, the Doge turned his attention towards the mainland with its Latin–Roman culture. As a result, Venetian culture changed focus, becoming more Roman than Byzantine, more Latin than Greek, while Carnival sought to recreate triumphal imperial processions. The triumphs of the Caesars became models for public spectacles. The new classical spirit was more emphatically present after 1527 when the Sack of Rome caused the migration of intellectuals and artists from the Eternal City to the *Nova Roma*, the peaceful and just Venice.

At moments you feel as if you are travelling in time

24

Peace and justice were the other components of the figural iconography of the Venetian myth. Since the Middle Ages artists had depicted Jurisprudence with references to King Solomon and the Emperor Trajan. Sometimes *Iustitia* took the form of a woman holding a scale, as in the arcade of the Palazzo Ducale or in a famous painting by Jacobello del Fiore. The Venetians constantly generated complex metaphorical imagery and visual icons that alluded to various female figures: the Mother of God and Venus, Rome and Troy, Justice and Beauty. These symbolic female allusions particularly impressed male visitors who referred to the city as a sensuous virgin queen.[3] The female citizens went so far as to masquerade as 'Venice' herself, a beautiful bejewelled woman with blonde hair.

Paolo Veronese, more significantly than other painters, combined various female personifications in his depiction of the city inside the Palazzo Ducale. In 1576 he was commissioned to paint an *Apotheosis of Venice* for the ceiling of the Sala del Maggior Consiglio, the hall in which foreign ambassadors and officials were received.[4] The painter portrayed the city as a beautiful female figure enthroned between Solomonic spiral columns, adored by her citizens and colonies. The monumental painting depicts a triumphal *bellissima donna* dressed in precious brocades, crowned by winged victories, majestically holding a sceptre. With his brush Veronese created a highly complex 'mask' of the city with all its subtle yet significant references and implications. For the most glorious festivities the concept of the 'Apotheosis of Venice,' with its visual focus on the Palazzo Ducale, symbolically extended beyond the confines of the palace. Temporary monumental architecture – floating theatres, triumphal arches and classical loggias – projected the theme into the most prominent spaces of the city and skywards into the cosmos. The Serenissima, as the peaceful and just Republic of Venice was described, celebrated its own primacy in the world by clothing herself with a female mask of splendour and triumph.

Architects, too, contributed in visualising the personified city, for they constructed the spatial context for the unfolding of spectacle and allegory. When Andrea Sansovino was commissioned by Doge Andrea Gritti to restore the Piazza and Piazzetta San Marco in the late 1520s he chose the symbolically charged classical style.[5] His *renovatio urbis* transformed the city's main space, with its older Byzantine and Gothic elements, into a Roman forum inspired by classical antiquity. His modifications to the urbanistic cityscape created a series of axial routes that visually link one monument to another. From the Basilica's central portal

The barrier between fiction and reality blurs under the effect of suggestion

25

Dangerous liaisons unfold in the
golden salons, boudoirs and
bedrooms of Venetian palazzos

A fascinating Marie Antoinette
promenades among the
corridors of a palazzo

Faces, postures and gestures
evoke the motto that the
movements of the body express
the movements of soul

to the extreme west of the Piazza (with the Church of San Gimignano, now the Correr Museum), from the columns of Mark and Theodore in the Piazzetta (forming the sea entrance to the Piazza proper) to Codussi's triumphal clock tower (under which one enters the commercial quarters of the city), from the Staircase of the Giants in the Palazzo Ducale courtyard to the Loggia abutting the Campanile, architects created conceptual, public and religious axes. The sacred, the civic and the spectacular were linked together by processional routes. The great Piazza, filled by Sansovino with *all'antica* motifs and structured with complex scenographic perspectives, was an ideal space for ceremony, pageantry and exhibition.

Andrea Palladio perfected Sansovino's ideas, extending the architectural scenography of the city toward the Basin of St Mark, while including the islands of the Giudecca and San Giorgio within one great panorama combining land and sea. The church of San Giorgio and the facade of the Redentore expanded the concept of triumph throughout the visible space from Piazza San Marco. Many other architectural projects, such as the building of a theatre–arena in the middle of the Lagoon, remained on paper.

Artists continued to perceive the city and her waters as a stage for civic ceremonies, religious liturgies and the reception of illustrious dignitaries. Narrative paintings such as Vittore Carpaccio's *Story of Saint Orsola*, Titian's *Presentation of the Virgin to the Temple*, and Paris Bordon's *Miracle of the Ring* depict historical and miraculous events before a triumphal backdrop. From Gritti's time onwards every major artistic or architectural project in some way incorporated the concept of the 'mask' of Venice. Thus, the governing authorities moulded the city into their own Utopian vision, especially during the days, weeks and months of Carnival.

Notes

1 For the religious, mythological and civic iconography of the Serenissima Republic see, D. Rosand, '*Venetia Figurata*: The Iconography of a Myth', in *Interpretazioni Veneziane: Studi di Storia dell'arte in onore di Michelangelo Muraro*, ed. D. Rosand (Venice, 1984), pp. 177–96; and, R. Goffen, *Piety and Patronage in Renaissance Venice: Bellini, Titian and the Franciscans* (New Haven and London, 1987), particularly the section about 'Venezia Vergine'.

2 P. Fortini Brown, *Venice and Antiquity* (New Haven and London, 1996).

3 For the comments of foreign visitors on Venice as female icon see, M.F. Rosenthal, *Veronica Franco, Citizen and Writer in Sixteenth Century Venice* (Chicago and London, 1992), especially the chapter 'Satirising the Courtesan: Franco's Enemies'.

4 Rosand, 1984. See also, A.C. Junkerman, 'Bellissima Donna: An Interdisciplinary Study of Venetian Sensuous Half-Length Images of the Early Sixteenth Century', PhD diss., University of California (Berkeley, 1988).

5 *Renovatio Urbis, Venezia nell'età di Andrea Gritti (1523-1538)*, ed. M. Tafuri (Rome, 1984).

An ambassador from Versailles

The Calendar of the Masks

Documents attest that the Venice Carnival recurred sporadically over a period of several months. Christmas marked the end of Advent and the day after 26 December, the feast of St Stephen, saw the beginning of the revelry. This was the official beginning of Carnival, which continued around the day of the Purification of Mary in January and ended on Shrove Tuesday, Mardi Gras, which usually falls between February and March. The climax of the masquerade on Shrove Thursday and the following Tuesday was contrasted by Ash Wednesday, which initiated the forty days of Lent. Surprisingly, the celebration was subsequently resumed after Easter, in June, in October and on many other festive occasions.

Carnival and Lent have always been perceived as polar opposites. The former is a time of indulgence and gluttony while the latter is a prolonged period of fasting and abstinence.[1] During Lent, Easter, Christmas and other important religious dates and Vesper hours, the wearing of masks was absolutely prohibited. However, Venetians were permitted to disguise themselves on days of the year that fell outside the traditional Carnival season: for the popular feast of the Ascension (*la Sensa*) in June and from early October to the 16 December. Special laws allowed the wearing of masks but forbade mourning during the most significant ducal ceremonies; for example, the coronation of the *dogaressa* (doge's wife), the reception of kings and queens or the arrival of ambassadors or important nobles. As one can imagine, urban spaces and waterways must have been filled with masked Venetians, beautiful decorated boats and jubilant visitors for approximately six months of every year.

On the feast of St Stephen a parade inaugurated the official Carnival in Piazza San Marco. After the doge had paid homage to the relics of the saint located on the island of San Giorgio, citizens, especially the patricians, exhibited their costumes and masks. In the Middle Ages this display took place in Campo Santo Stefano but from the fifteenth century it was moved to Piazza San Marco, a far more appropriate backdrop for such an event. The parade of costumes was called the *Liston,* as was the monumental Venetian catwalk under the Procuratie's porticoes where the procession took place. From the very beginning these processions were characterised by exhibitionism and excess in spite of the modesty and decorum constantly advised by the state. The display of luxury reached such a climax during the early Renaissance that by the sixteenth century the Republic was forced to enact a series of sumptuary laws generally actualised only in the eighteenth century. Full social equality, as manifest in dress, was never achieved despite the government regulation.

La Nature est un temple où de vivants piliers laissent parfois sortir de confuses paroles:
L'homme y passe à travers des forêts des symboles qui l'observent avec des regards familiers.

(Baudelaire, 'Correspondances')

In the weeks following the feast of St Stephen the Venetians celebrated the Purification of Mary with great devotion. Although it was forbidden to wear masks during most of the sacred feasts, the days immediately before and after the Purification were an exception because at that time of the year the Republic needed simultaneously to commemorate the sacred and the civic. In fact, the celebration climaxed with the eight-day festival of the Twelve Marys,[2] a medieval feast that survived in one form or another until the end of the Republic. The name 'Twelve Marys' refers to the twelve sacred statues that were publicly exhibited in the palaces of the nobles before being transported by boat in a procession to the three cathedrals: San Pietro a Castello, San Marco and Santa Maria Formosa. The identification of Mary's virginity with the city's purity was especially emphasised in the festival by the remembrance of a specific historical event, namely the rescue of Venetian virgins kidnapped by pirates. For this reason the Twelve Marys evolved into a public spectacle in which the government presented twelve beautiful Venetian girls with dowries, long considered essential for marriage. From 1379 the festival of the Twelve Marys became increasingly civic in character and consequently came to be more in keeping with the atmosphere of masquerade. The Purification as a whole was a celebration of Venetian purity and beauty and as such strongly highlighted the pious quality of the Republic.

Shrove Thursday and Tuesday were the most important dates in the Carnival calendar. During the so-called *settimana grassa*[3] (Shrove week) Piazza San Marco, Campo Santo Stefano and the Basin of San Marco hosted the main celebrations while the *campi*, *calli* and bridges were destined for more popular events. In this period Carnival took the form of eccentric masquerades, bullfights, animal tortures, acrobatic human flights and performances, battles on bridges, regattas, dances, epithalamic celebrations, comedies, allegorical spectacles and fantastic fireworks. These were the last moments of joy before the imminent purgation of Lent. Shrove Tuesday had always represented the threshold of Lent, so much so that in the eighteenth century, while the people burned the gigantic Pantalon – a mask in the form of the King of Anarchy – and shouted their adieu with the famous exclamation 'El va! El va! El va! El carneval el va!', the religious authorities hastily prepared a pulpit for prayer in between the columns of the Piazzetta.[4] The last hours of Carnival were the most emotional moment for the revellers and were meant to evoke both the sacred and the profane.

The Ascension of Christ was a religious and civic feast held in June that resumed the joy which had preceded Lent. On Ascension Day 1177, Doge Sebastiano Ziani hosted the famous reconciliation between Pope Alexander III and Frederick Barbarossa. Although the Doge merely acted as an arbiter for the meeting, he claimed the same status as the Pope and the Holy Roman Emperor, as if together they formed a triad of European power. In recognition of its role, the Pope gave Venice the right to celebrate the Ascension with a civic ritual that became dear to all her citizens: the Betrothal to the Sea. Central to this ceremony was the *desponsatio maris*, the wedding with the Adriatic, in which the doge threw a ring into the Lagoon as a symbol of the eternal and mystical marriage between the water and the city. A cortege of boats with nobles and citizens in costume watched the symbolic act of union, which was celebrated for many days with spectacles and masquerades, receptions and games, continuing through the summer into autumn.

From the feast of St Stephen to Shrove Tuesday, from the Ascension to late autumn, Venetians inhabited a dream world in which, both consciously and unconsciously, they commemorated the power, expansion and justice of their serene Republic.[5]

Notes

1. Throughout Europe the battle between Carnival and Lent was represented allegorically by the ringing of bells on the evening of Shrove Tuesday, symbolically ending the time of laughter with a message of penance. Throughout the forty days of Lent masks were strictly forbidden.

2. E. Muir, *Civic Ritual in Renaissance Venice* (Princeton, N.J, 1981), p. 154–55. My analysis of religious and civic celebrations in Venice is based on Muir's studies. See also G. Reiner-Michiel, *Origine delle Feste Veneziane*, 6 vols (Milan, 1829).

3. B. Sorsi, *La Settimana Grassa* (Venice, 1677).

4. D. Reato, *Storia del Carnevale di Venezia* (Venice, 1991), pp. 114–15.

5. The best studies on the Venetian Carnival are: A. Giurgea, 'Theatre of the Flesh: The Carnival of Venice and the Theatre of the World', PhD diss., University of California (Los Angeles, 1987); and D. Reato, *Storia del Carnevale di Venezia* (Venice, 1991); then follows: E. Vittoria, *Venezia Festa del Carnevale. Origine e Storia* (Venice, 1980); P. Correnti, *Il Carnevale di Venezia* (Milan, 1968); G. Mariacher, *Il Carnevale a Venezia* (Venice, 1966). Both Giurgea and Reato analyse numerous documents and images in order to reconstruct the spirit of Carnival between the Middle Ages and the Napoleonic invasion. Paintings, engravings, laws, statutes and so on, help the authors to investigate the celebrations of the Carnival in Venice. Giurgea's dissertation, written in Venice in the years of the Carnival revival in the 1980s, is not a mere analysis of the actual rituals and celebrations but a conceptual study embracing the philosophy behind the Republic's organisation of the Carnival. Undoubtedly, Giurgea's dissertation is the best study of the subject and consequently has been the main source of inspiration for my essay.

Architecture and masks
complement each other in the
City's alluring piazzas

Waft on the breeze, or sink in clouds of gold;
Transparent forms, too fine for mortal sight,
Their fluid bodies half dissolved in light.
Loose to the wind their airy garments flew.

(Alexander Pope, 'The Rape of the Lock')

  Thin glittering textures of the filmy dew;
Dipped in the richest tinctures of the skies,
Where light disports in ever-mingling dyes.

(Alexander Pope, 'The Rape of the Lock')

Violence and Spectacle

In Venice, violence was a form of spectacle that involved animals and human beings. Fights, tortures, acrobatic exercises and dangerous games transformed Piazza San Marco into an arena, with the contestants as protagonists of a show applauded by the doge in person. With these events the Venetians celebrated their physical strength, courageous spirit and historical victories and welcomed illustrious visitors.

Between the fifteenth and seventeenth centuries animals were the unlucky protagonists of most of the amusements.[1] Sixteenth-century records claim that stags, geese, cats, bears, dogs and, above all, bulls were tortured to death in the piazzas. These morbid shows took place in Piazza San Marco, Campo Santo Stefano, San Polo, Santa Margherita, San Geremia, Santa Maria Formosa and other public spaces. An engraving of 1610 by Giacomo Franco illustrating the *Habiti d'huomini et donne venetiane* (*Costumes of Venetian Men and Women*) depicts animal torture during a festivity. The setting is recognisable as Campo Santa Maria Formosa, where a great variety of animals were displayed. In the right foreground a goose, its legs tied, is suspended upside down above a canal next to a bridge. The image suggests that the game involved jumping from the bridge in order to grab the long neck of the bird. To the left a cat can be seen tied with its back against a wooden panel, its legs partially free to move. A man wearing a skull on his head repeatedly bites the stomach of the cat which reacts by scratching the skull. Just behind this cruel scene a chained bear is attacked by dogs, directed by men who were often obliged to bite the dogs' tails in order to detach them from the huge animal's body. Concern was expressed for the dogs but never the bear who was always the main victim. The same can be said of the ducks tied on top of a wooden column to the right of the engraving and the bulls being victimised in the background. Bulls were subjected to much cruelty including *tauromachia*.

A number of spectacles commemorated political victories by sacrificing animals. In 1162 Ulrich the German Patriarch of Aquileia, taking advantage of the fact that Venice was at war on the mainland, invaded Grado, a Venetian subject town, with the assistance of his Friulian allies. The *fabri* (the ironworkers' guild), supported by the doge's artillery, fought against Ulrich and was able to retake Grado. The Patriarch was imprisoned along with twelve of his canons and later obliged to pay a yearly tribute to the Republic of a bull and twelve pigs. In a ceremony re-enacting the event the thirteen animals were convicted by state magistrates in a trial held at the Palazzo Ducale. The animals were then slaughtered

The Venice Carnival has a melancholic essence, a spleen that recalls the poems of Baudelaire

by a member of the *fabri*, whose skill was measured by his ability to decapitate the beasts. The aim was to cut off their heads with a single stroke without his sword touching the ground. To conclude the ceremony, miniature castles representing the neighbouring Friuli cities exploded in fireworks symbolising the power of Venice over its colonies and enemies.

While San Marco was the setting for more solemn spectacles the smaller *campi* were stages for extremely cruel bullfights. Unlike the Spanish *corrida*, the Venetian bullfight was a contest between bulls and dogs.[2] The human element was limited to training the dogs and restraining the bulls with ropes during the event. The unfortunate animal, tied by its horns and anchored to the ground, was held fast by volunteers called *tiratori*, who were dressed in black and white and wore hats exhibiting the colours of their district. They held the bulls firmly while the *cavacani* (dog trainers) stimulated the dogs' rage. Often men intervened to protect the dogs or prevent the bulls from charging into the cheering crowds. Others had the responsibility of preserving the bull carcasses after the event in order to avoid paying a fine to the butchers who were to sell the meat. The fights coincided with the day before the meat market and were announced with great pomp. The *campi* were even provided with seats for hundreds, if not thousands, of spectators who shouted to the *tiratori* and *cavacani*. In their cruelty the Venetians went so far as to set off fireworks around the dying animal's horns. As in ancient Roman times, such behaviour was a significant part of public spectacle, but it did not go completely unopposed.

Some Venetians did not approve of the bloody events. In his written account Michele Battagia reveals the revulsion of these citizens to the cruelty of the bullfights.[3] The Republic implemented a series of laws to curb them, but they were not fully prohibited until the post-Republican era. In the seventeenth century the Council of Ten forbade the *tiratori* from leading bulls through the streets of Venice; sometimes the frightened animals harmed the crowd.[4] The same council persistently attempted to protect the citizenry by limiting violence to the animals but the macabre spectacles remained very popular throughout all Carnivals. Only during the Napoleonic and Austrian occupations were the fights suppressed.

Truly mesmerising must have been the acrobatic performances of the *Forze d'Ercole* (Herculean labours) in the Piazzetta San Marco, which increased in difficulty and danger over the course of the eighteenth century.[5] A painting by Gabriel Bella in the Querini Stampalia affords a glimpse of what the *Forze d'Ercole* must have been like.[6] It depicts a

Masked characters waiting for a
gondola on the Grand Canal

41

human pyramid, each man standing on the shoulders, head, back, feet or stomach of the one below. The pyramid was usually assembled on a stage, but sometimes it was formed on a floating platform or even on ice when the Lagoon had frozen over. Each acrobat had a task that corresponded to his weight, body structure and level of skill. The men at the base (*saorna*) of the pyramid were called *sforzanti* and supported the entire human assembly. The summit (*cimiereto*) was often completed by a child, who upon reaching his goal some twenty metres above the ground, waved a victory flag high above the gathered masses. Each movement was carefully calculated in order not to destabilise the fragile human structure. The acrobats formed not only triangular compositions but increasingly difficult assemblages with sophisticated names: Union, House of Mohammed, Beautiful Venice, Lion, Three Bridges, Colossus of Rhodes, Foundation of Thoughts, Glory, Superb Emperor and many others. These complex forms reminded the Venetians of their colonies, the city's social and economic relations with Islam, the glory of Venice and, especially, the courage and skill of their fellow citizens.

Daring and difficulty in acrobatics intensified in competitions between the districts. Venice was divided into six *sestrieri* – San Marco, Castello, Dorsoduro, San Polo, Santa Croce and Cannareggio. However, the population divided itself more or less evenly into two groups: the Castellani and Nicolotti. The Castellani lived in the three *sestrieri* around San Marco and were represented principally by the workers of the naval industries in the Arsenal, the main shipyard of the Republic. The Nicolotti, geographically located between Rialto and Cannareggio, identified with the fishermen of San Nicolò dei Mendicoli and the merchants of the Rialto. The Castellani and Nicolotti competed against each other in acrobatics, victory symbolically asserting the primacy of one group over the other.

The intense rivalry between the two factions had its origins in the twelfth-century war between Ulrich and the Republic. An account from that time states that the Castellani and Nicolotti had specific roles in the conquest of Grado: the Castellani formed human ladders to scale the city walls while the Nicolotti breached the Patriarch's stronghold. Emotionally charged re-enactments were performed before the Venetian citizens.

The Castellani and Nicolotti actually came to blows at times, particularly between October and Christmas. Fist fights, known as 'Battles of the Bridges', took place on strategic bridges throughout the city: Ponte dei Carmini, dei Servi, della Guerra, San Marziale, de

The sun illuminates the masks of
Piazza San Marco before nightfall,
when fog changes every form into
an evanescent vision

Gesuati, Santa Sofia and San Barnaba. These violent confrontations are documented as early as 1295. The tension between the two factions led to bloodshed on more than one occasion, especially when the numerous spectators threw themselves into the mêlée. Although in the eighteenth century the state attempted to outlaw the battles, it tolerated them to a certain degree because of their value in preparing young Venetians for real warfare. Castellani and Nicolotti also challenged each other in spectacular regattas that filled the Lagoon with a festive parade of ships, and in dancing the *moresca*, a dagger dance in seven movements that symbolised the struggle against the Turks.[7] Carnival spectacles were filled with metaphorical connotations alluding to historical or symbolic events.

The Castellani had an opportunity to show off their skill in the presence of the doges. In addition to the *Forze d'Ercole*, trained acrobats among the Arsenal workers (*arsenalotti*) walked a tightrope between the waters of the dock and the top of the Campanile, so that they were suspended high above the Piazzetta San Marco. The enthroned doge, all the officials of the Republic and thousands of spectators seated on temporary bleachers, gazed in awe as the performers, risking death, ascended and descended the rope. According to legend the hazardous spectacle had been introduced into the city by a Turk who climbed atop the Campanile on a tightrope anchored to a boat in the Basin of San Marco. Hence the performance was called the 'Flight of the Turk' or the 'Flight of the Angel', until a dove-shaped puppet replaced the acrobats in the final years. Carnival today is inaugurated with the '*Volo della Colombina*' (the 'Flight of the Dove').

The sixteenth and eighteenth centuries saw the 'Flight of the Angel' become an increasingly breathtaking exhibition of skill, precision and beauty. The 'angels', as the Arsenal workers were called during their acrobatics on the rope, were able to reach the doge's throne with a bouquet of flowers, a madrigal, a poem or a song. One of them ascended from below the water of the Basin, rising above the waves to the top of the Campanile's lantern disguised as Neptune. Cristoforo Ivanovich took pains to record the name of Sante di Ca da Lezze, whose incredible skill above the Piazzetta in 1680 and 1681 earned him a special place in history.[8] Sante literally flew, first on a horse and then on a boat, both being manoeuvred on a series of ropes from the Lagoon to the very top of the Campanile and back. Animals, acrobats and wrestlers animated the public spaces of the city while more esoteric celebrations took place in Venetian noble residences.

C'est la mort qui console, hélas! et qui fait vivre;
C'est le but de la vie, et c'est le seul espoir
Qui, comme un élixir, nous monte et nous enivre,
Et nous donne le coeur de marcher jusqu'au soir . . .

(Baudelaire, 'La Mort des Pauvres')

45

Notes

1 D. Reato, *Storia del Carnevale di Venezia* (Venice, 1991), especially pp. 35–41.

2 For more information about Venetian bullfights see M. Battagia, *Cicalata sulle Cacce di Tori Veneziani* (Venice, 1844).

3 Ibid. pp. 30–31.

4 E A. Cicogna, *Delle Inscrizioni Veneziane raccolte ed illustrate da E. A. C.* (Venice, 1824–53), vol. 3, p. 467.

5 D. Reato, 1991, pp. 23–34. See also A. Pilot, 'Un Episodio Tragico di Forze d'Ercole a Venezia nel 1810', *Rivista d'Italia*, July 1915, pp. 68–72.

6 A. Zorzi, 'Serenissima Ludens. Giochi Veneziani nelle tele di Gabriel Bella', *FMR*, 11, 1983, pp. 84–87; *I Giochi Veneziani del Settecento nei Dipinti di Gabriel Bella*, catalogue by M. Gemin and E. Merkel (Venice, 1978); and B. Tamassia Mazzarotto, *Le Feste Veneziane. I Giochi Popolari, le Cerimonie Religiose e di Governo illustrate da Gabriel Bella* (Florence, 1961).

7 The *moresca* is an extremely difficult dance in seven acts: *Azion, alle Prime, Tagioturco, Zenociada, le Passae, la Sottogamba, il Disarmo*. The movements symbolise the fight against the Turks, re-enacted by the Castellani and Nicolotti from the fifteenth to the eighteenth centuries. Interestingly, this dance is performed on the Island of Korcula near the Dalmatian coast. In March 1983 the inhabitants of the island retaught the Venetians of Piazza San Marco how to dance the *moresca*. See L. Padoan Urban, *La Moresca. Danze carnevalesche e mimiche antiche Veneziane* (Vicenza, 1983).

8 C. Ivanovich, *Minerva al tavolino . . . con Memorie teatrali di Venezia* (Venice, 1681), pp. 380–81.

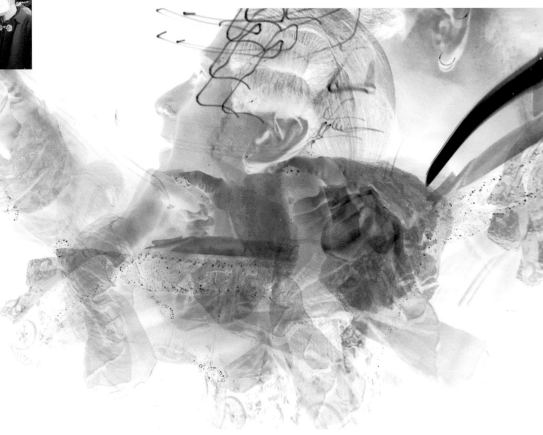

But sleep did not afford me respite from thought and misery; my dreams presented a thousand objects that scared me. Towards morning I was possessed by a kind of nightmare; I felt the fiend's grasp in my neck, and could not free myself from it; groans and cries rung in my ears.

(Mary Shelley, *Frankenstein*)

The masks of Piazza San Marco
manifest time, the elements,
mysteries and feelings with the
esoteric language of allegory

Humanist Theatre

Many Venetians waited all year for the festive atmosphere of Shrove Thursday to announce publicly their engagements or weddings during traditional epithalamic celebrations called *mumarie*.[1] The word *mumaria* probably derives from mimes that incorporated humour into a mythological fable of marriage. For these occasions the salons of the patrician palaces were decorated with damask, brocade, silk, oriental rugs, mirrors and glass of all colours, with torches on the main facade. The ritual began in front of the bride's window where the groom would honour his future wife. After accepting his marriage proposal she received a precious ring as a symbol of his faithful promise. This would be followed by her dancing a special minuet as a sign of her love. A Carnival spirit immediately took over when actors mocked the betrothed in a burlesque display. This continued throughout the day in a series of pantomimes, which spread from the privacy of the family palace into the piazzas. Nobles and citizens alike participated in the fun, following the couple from their home through the thronging spaces of the city.

The richest families in Venice liked to associate themselves with ancient gods and heroes, inventing a connection of noble lineage with classical Greece and Rome.[2] Thus, the adventures of Hercules, the Judgement of Paris, the fables of Meleager or Jason and the Golden Fleece were incorporated into the *mumarie* alluding to the families of the betrothed couple. The spirit of these wedding celebrations legitimised the institution of nobility and at the same time contributed to the fun and public mayhem of Carnival. In spite of its epithalamic connotation the word *mumaria* also referred to any kind of allegorical spectacle involving mimes or actors.

Renaissance Venice was one of the main centres for text printing; its culture was dominated by an extremely refined elite and revolved around the many books published by Aldo Manuzio. The more cultivated *mumarie* or *fabulae*, as they were also called, could be extremely eclectic, often adopting styles in the spirit of the poems published in the city itself and beyond. The courtly poetry of Angelo Poliziano, Matteo Maria Boiardo and Ludovico Ariosto and above all the famous late-fifteenth-century illustrated text *Hypnerotomachia Poliphili* by Francesco Colonna, were among these. Less cultivated and more spectacular *mumarie* could involve pastoral, chivalric, Christian and pagan themes simultaneously. Nymphs, satyrs, devils and gods were the protagonists of a fantasy world in which purity, beauty and culture were rhetorically juxtaposed with ugliness, barbarity and ignorance.

52

One project for a *mumaria* written for the Piazza San Marco called for a particularly eclectic spectacle.[3] The script was based on the theme of love as seen through a variety of antitheses: rusticity and civilisation, forest and palace, brutality and grace, imprisonment and freedom, beauty and the grotesque. Its author conceived a stage supporting a palace, a small hill, a garden and a forest. A group of actors impersonated two giant guardians beside the palace, Cupid inside the hill, his mother Venus–Selene on top of the hill, nymphs in the garden and wild men and untamed animals in the forest. In an unspecified location there were also six knights on horseback. Surprising the spectators, the show began with Cupid coming out of the mountain to pay homage to Venus. He joined the beautiful nymphs in the garden who, during a dance, were suddenly attacked by the wild men and taken into the forest. Here the giants kidnapped the most beautiful of the nymphs and tied her to a tree in front of the palace. What followed was a rapid sequence of scenes in which the nymphs and other protagonists were repeatedly liberated and recaptured. These were interspersed with spectacular battles among animals, giants, wild men and knights complemented with fireworks and explosions. As in a *psychomachia*, good triumphed over evil and love over hatred. In the end, the knights awakened by Cupid embraced the nymphs and participated in a victorious cavalcade around Piazza San Marco led by Venus and her son seated on a unicorn.

These spectacles could take various forms and meanings involving satire, music and dance performed by masked characters. The so-called *mascarate* were aristocratic satires based on courtly poetry and Carnival dances such as the *quodlibet*, the *moresca* and the *villotta*. In 1590 the Venetian Giovanni Croce, the leader of the Cappella di San Marco, composed music for the *Mascarate Piacevoli et Ridicolose per il Carnevale*,[4] originally written by an anonymous poet and then held in a collection by the nobleman Leonardo Sanudo. Croce's compositions were specifically intended for the Venetian Knights of St John of Malta and were performed in their monastery theatre as *intermedii* between the acts of comedies and banquets, but the *mascarate* were popular entertainments among the aristocracy in theatres and palaces throughout Carnival. Significantly, Croce's characters allude to nobles, courtesans and foreigners, often disguised as lower-class people who, through parody and irony, satirised Venetian society. The *mascarate* often invoked and emphasised the myth of the Serenissima and criticised the inappropriate behaviour of

nobles and visitors to Venice. As explained by Jenon Gustafson Donnamae, these theatrical plays might have been manipulated by those in power in order to maintain social propriety and convey a political message.[5] The Republic could control Carnival shows with a certain authority in order to maintain the *ordene antiguo* and decorum.

The invention and planning of humanist spectacles was entrusted to specialised associations of cultivated nobles called the *compagnie della calza*.[6] Officially recognised in 1400, these clubs, composed of young aristocrats distinguished by their coloured hose (*calza*), evolved into private institutions with their own laws and jurisdictions. The difference between these *compagnie*, whose members had a solid humanist education, and other Carnival associations was mainly cultural. The intellectually inclined *compagnie* produced esoteric pageants enhanced with classical anecdotes, legends and allegory. In addition, they used their wealth to commission famous artists to decorate theatres and writers to create sophisticated texts.

The *compagnie* were charged with controlling the Carnival's festivities, which might otherwise have fallen into chaos and disorder. Each member was entrusted to use vigilance and creativity to maintain order within the revelry. The duties assumed by the young members served as a valuable training for their future careers as officials of the Republic when similar skills were transferred from the realm of Carnival to that of the state administration. The hierarchical structure of the *compagnie* reflected that of the ducal government. The leader of each *compagnia* was known as the 'prior', under whom served an administrator (*sindaco*), a treasurer (*camerlengo*) and a number of counsellors. There were many associations called '*della calza*' (*degli Immortali, dei Fedeli, degli Accesi, dei Potenti, dei Sempiterni*) each of which, by law, was composed exclusively of aristocratic youth. Since their members were required to be under a certain age the groups tended to disband after only a few years of operation, only to resurface under a new name with fresh members. In the second half of the sixteenth century the power of the *compagnie* was radically curtailed as they became elite private clubs with no real authority.

One of the earliest (late fifteenth century) visual representations of the members of the *compagnie della calza* and the ephemeral theatrical structures for which they were responsible is Vittorio Carpaccio's cycle of paintings for the Scuola di Sant' Orsola, a Venetian lay confraternity. In the pictorial cycles, known as the *teleri*, the most significant

56

images are those of arriving and departing emissaries who pass before fantastic architectural backdrops similar to those constructed specially for the Carnival celebrations. Art historians have long debated the meaning of Carpaccio's complex symbolic architecture (circular temples, triumphal arches and loggias), which does not seem to relate to the way Venice must have looked in the fifteenth century. However, links have been made between buildings in Jerusalem, Damascus, Constantinople, Cairo, Alexandria and Rome and those in Carpaccio's paintings. Art historians have also compared the latter to the projects of Mauro Codussi and Pietro Lombardo, the two most important Venetian architects of the early Renaissance. Seldom have art historians considered the possibility that the structures in Carpaccio's paintings were in fact temporary buildings created for the reception of foreign dignitaries and would have been discarded after use. We know from documentary sources that most of this ephemeral architecture was designed and decorated by famous artists. For example, diarists and chronicles testify that Andrea Palladio, Vincenzo Scamozzi, Camillo Rusconi, Titian, Paolo Veronese, Jacopo Tintoretto and others participated in the construction of a chimerical Venice that existed only during the days of celebrations. As for Carpaccio, Patricia Fortini Brown intelligently argues that the world he depicts in his visual narrative: 'is not what Venetians saw but what they wished to see'[7] – a veritable Utopia. Utopia was given tangible form at Carnival through masks, art and architecture.

The *Theatrum Mundi* or 'Theatre of the World', was the epitome of Venetian temporary architecture.[8] It consisted of a floating round wooden structure that functioned as a true theatre and included a *scenae* for the actors and a *cavea* for the spectators. In addition, it served as an open stage on which actors, singers and musicians welcomed arriving foreign dignitaries. Visible from waterfronts, bridges, palaces and passing boats, the movement of the theatre facilitated interaction between citizens and actors, life and fiction.

The Theatre of the World used allegorical symbolism derived primarily from its physical form. From the fifteenth to the eighteenth centuries the *Theatrum* evolved as an experiment on the esoteric significance of a circular platform on which atlantes, caryatids and talamones supported a cupola and a sphere-shaped lantern. Mythological and astrological decoration added to the metaphorical meanings of the floating theatre, which was often compared to the Earth, the ocean, a constellation or the enigmas of philosophy symbolised in its spherical shape. Neoplatonic thinking and mystical geometry emphasise that the

The desire to live the past is one of the
spirits that animates the Venice Carnival

The festival also explores fantasy
expressed in colours and forms that
are the product of the imagination

Two 'bautte' walking in the
meandering alleyways of Venice

60

circle has neither beginning nor end. The fact that all points on its perimeter are equidistant from the centre illustrates the unity, infinity, justice and uniformity of the cosmos and its divine ruler. The mystical geometry of the circle and sphere gave architectural forms a transcendental significance and helped catalyse the later astronomical discoveries of two important figures: Nicolas Copernicus and Galileo.

Mystical geometry was based on ancient mathematics, philosophy and medieval theology, all of which were revived and reinterpreted in Renaissance thought and architecture. Pythagoras, Parmenides, Plato, Plotinus, Paracelsus, Boethius, Dionysius the Aeropagite, St Augustine, St Thomas Aquinas and Dante formed the basis for a complex order of ideas that, generally speaking, viewed the cosmos and eternity as a sphere with man at the centre. Nicolas of Cusa, Marsilio Ficino, Pico della Mirandola, Copernicus and Blaise Pascal reworked ancient ideas into a new system that subtly blended hermeticism, cabalism, astral cosmology, Neoplatonic thought and science. Renaissance thinkers believed that the universe could be measured geometrically, just as mystery could be explained and represented allegorically. Such thinking was manifest in the ideal round-shaped temple regarded by Leon Battista Alberti as the perfect form. Palladio and Sebastiano Serlio further developed these mathematical and aesthetic concepts into a complex architectural theory. The round structure, which they called *Theatrum Mundi*, mirrored the cosmos and represented the secrets of the world with its man-made metaphorical spectacles. As Adrian Giurgea explains, to its cultivated spectators each performance was a ritual and, as in a secret rite, the theatre itself was burned at the end.[9] Thus, one could define the Theatre of the World as a mystical structure floating on the Lagoon, a symbolic building with actors communicating in an esoteric language of word and gesture; the glory of the Serenissima and its relationship with eternity and the universe. Architecture and drama simultaneously imitated history, the world, time, the cosmos and Venice itself. 'The floating theatres of Venice were symbolic reductions of the entire universe to the space of the city. In the liturgical and secular space of the Carnival the allegories of integration to the cosmic order celebrated the divine constitution of the Serenissima', her inhabitants 'seeing and admiring themselves.'[10]

The appearance of the Theatre of the World in the fifteenth and sixteenth centuries occurred when the Venetian mainland, more than the city of Venice itself, was becoming an experimental centre for philosophy, architecture and theatre. The beautiful town of Asolo developed into a centre of northern Italian humanism in the years around 1500. Queen Caterina Cornaro created a highly cultivated court that included the likes of Pietro Bembo, Giorgione and Sannazaro, who were committed to the exploration of pastoral and hermetic themes in music, painting and poetry. In the second half of the sixteenth century a sophisticated elite created a complex and fascinating culture in which esoteric thought combined the Graeco-Roman and Judaeo-Christian worlds. Daniele Barbaro, a Venetian noble who lived in the splendour of Villa Maser, was probably the best known member of the cultivated thinkers who conceptually combined architecture, painting, theatre and philosophy.[11]

Giulio Camillo Delminio, who travelled among several Italian cities in the second half of the sixteenth century, explored neoplatonic ideas in *L'Idea del teatro*. In Delminio's complex thinking, the Theatre of the World is a combination of astrological symbols that celebrate the dignity of man, a mnemonic invention based on Platonic archetypes yet strongly rooted in reality. Reality played an important role in Delminio's text because his main purpose was to unlock the mysteries of nature through real discourse. If viewed within this sophisticated context the Theatre of the World reveals itself as a distinctly esoteric form of communication specifically addressed to *cognoscenti* and illustrious visitors.

More than any other Italian or European state the Serenissima had a long tradition of welcoming distinguished visitors for whom the Republic created the spectacle of Carnival and masked the entire city as a beautiful and democratic queen.[12] Members of the Este, Gonzaga and Savoy families, holy Roman emperors, cardinals, kings and emperors all visited the Lagoon and were received with great pomp and ceremony. Most of these visits related to the city's position as the main point of departure for Jerusalem, an expensive pilgrimage destination affordable only to the very rich. Venice had always been the gateway to the Orient and the home of the largest military fleet for the defence of Constantinople and Jerusalem. It was also the starting point for many crusades to the Holy Land, causing the city often to be compared and identified with Jerusalem. The journey to Palestine was especially perilous because of violent storms and the omnipresent Turkish threat. Venetian mariners effectively protected and escorted the pilgrims down the Adriatic and across the open sea. The city authorities turned pilgrimage, which started in the Basilica of San Marco and ended at the Church of the Holy Sepulchre in Jerusalem, into a veritable industry.

Aristocratic pilgrims were recommended to the doges or high city officials by their lords back home, thus animating the diplomatic activity between Venice and other nations.

As the visits became commonplace the state created a standardised official programme that could be adjusted according to the nobility of the visitors, their country of provenance and the significance of their mission. In the eighteenth century a typical diplomatic reception could last four days. On the first day the guests were welcomed by the doge and his most important subordinates with a theatrical procession of ships. After exchanging gifts, often precious costumes, guests were accompanied to their quarters. The next day they witnessed a regatta and other public shows and then attended a formal dinner at the Palazzo Ducale. The following days were spent on a guided tour of Venice which included the Basilica, the Palazzo Ducale, the Arsenal and the Treasury of St Mark. The state aimed to instil in its distinguished guests an appreciation for the sacredness of the city, the opulence of the citizens and the power of the fleet and artillery.

When Beatrice d'Este, wife of the Duke of Milan, visited Venice she was received in grand style.[13] In a letter to her husband she describes a floating chariot representing the personification of Justice, accompanied by an ox (symbol of the city of Milan), St Mark (patron saint and protector of Venice) and a serpent (a pejorative representation of the papacy, against which the Republic was at war). She goes on to describe a triumphal arch made of palm fronds and olive leaves with a huge bust of il Moro, the Milanese duke. The Duchess, awed by such splendour, explains to her husband that the message of the theatrical allegory was directed to his Excellency the Duke of Milan, author of peace and tranquillity and ally of the Venetian Republic. The elaborate *fabula* achieved the Republic's aim, to flatter and impress the ducal family with an unambiguous political message.

The arrival of Federico Gonzaga, Duke of Mantua, was celebrated with an even more ostentatious *Theatrum Mundi*[14] constructed on pontoons in front of Palazzo Foscari where the Duke was lodged. The theatre, supported by fantastic seahorses, was illuminated by servants holding torches. Actors and mimers performed a *mumaria* filled with allusions to the building and subsequent burning of Troy. The theatrical play included figures riding fanciful animals, allegories of giants, and even a Laocoon strangled by snakes. The drama glorified the Gonzaga family, highlighting its origins in antiquity. Only a highly cultivated man able to grasp the subtle allegorical and symbolic meanings could have fully appreciated the

Allegories, spirits, creatures of the imagination

production. Nevertheless, the less educated masses would certainly have been impressed.

Renaissance masquerades were permeated by strong political messages. In 1572, after the victory of Venice against the Turks at Lepanto, a cortege celebrated the event with great ardour.[15] Triumphal chariots displayed symbols and narratives: Faith slaying a dragon; the Theological Virtues; personifications of Rome, Spain and Venice (participants in the battle); Victory, Charity and Death. Amidst all this, a group of defeated Turkish soldiers were chained together and humiliated. Princely families such as the Medici in Florence, Montefeltro in Urbino, Este in Ferrara and Gonzaga in Mantua often sought to revive the spirit of ancient Roman successes, known through numerous textual sources and celebrated in Petrarch's famous work, *The Triumphs*.

The most elaborate of all Venetian celebrations took place during the visit of Henry III on 17 July 1574.[16] Henry had been crowned King of Poland in Krakow and was travelling around the Continent before his return to Paris, where he was to be crowned King of France. Stopping in Venice for a brief sojourn during Carnival, he found awaiting him one of the most spectacular welcomes in the history of the Republic, which secretly hoped to establish an alliance with the future ruler. On his way to the Veneto from Eastern Europe the King was joined by Venetian envoys in Friuli and escorted in a jubilant procession all the way to the Lagoon. From there he was accompanied to the Grand Canal by dozens of ships carrying hundreds of actors performing allegories of welcome while multitudes of spectators applauded from lavishly decorated balconies and platforms.

A huge triumphal arch built by Palladio and decorated by Tintoretto and Veronese had been constructed on the water between the Basin of San Marco and the Lido. This elegant structure, modelled on the arch of Septimius Severus in Rome, was linked to a floating classical loggia exhibiting an allegory of Henry's deeds. Loggias were used by the city as venues for musical performances, but on this occasion the structure assumed the dignity of a sacred temple. Behind the portico the patriarch blessed the future King of France before an altar. After the blessing Henry boarded the *Bucintoro*, the enormous ducal boat, and proceeded to Palazzo Foscari where his lodgings had been prepared. For ten days the King admired regattas and water parades organised in his honour, dining in the most splendid palaces using tablecloths, napkins, plates and forks made of sugar and witnessing the passage of the Theatres of the World along the Grand Canal and the explosion of

65

Sacred and profane: the bell tower
and a demon

A stroll before the Procuratie Vecchie

An eighteenth-century gentleman
sets out for the ball

68

fireworks while enjoying the company of the legendary courtesan Veronica Franco.[17]

Venice had been at the heart of a vast allegory of coronation, which had begun in Krakow and would continue to Paris. Yet for the Venetians the public spectacles represented the latest political alliance in a dangerous new Europe where the northern superpowers invaded the weaker Italian city states. In spite of the imminent threat from beyond the Alps the Republic of the Serenissima continued its happy Utopian introversion.

By the eighteenth century the Atlantic Ocean had long usurped the ancient role of the Mediterranean. The primacy of the Republic as a commercial centre was rivalled by Spanish, Portuguese and other north-European ports. Rich and decadent Venice feared both an economic crisis and a foreign invasion. Under these circumstances it was only natural that it would seek powerful allies such as the future Russian tsar.

The arrival in1782 of Paul Petrovich, future Emperor Paul I of Russia and his wife Maria Fedorovna, saw the last great diplomatic reception before the end of the Republic.[18] They arrived in January at the height of the Carnival festivities. Petrovich and his wife were known by the alias 'Count and Countess from the North' because they preferred to travel incognito. Venetian officials met them in Udine where they had been lodging in the archbishop's palace, discreetly disguised as a hotel. At Conegliano, on the Venetian mainland, the noble couple was received with great honour by the envoy Giovanni Grimani and Francesco Pesaro, procurator of the state. Discretion gave way to frenzied pomp when the party came within sight of the Lagoon. Although the couple refused to travel on the glorious ship prepared for them by the Serenissima, they were nevertheless accompanied by hundreds of boats, gondolas and floating platforms as far as the Rialto, where masked Venetians applauded their arrival. On entering the Piazza San Marco the welcome became overtly triumphal. In front of the church of San Gimignano, demolished by Napoleon less than two decades later, Venetian architects had reproduced the facade of the noble residence of St Petersburg and a classical arch similar to that of Titus in the Roman Forum. That evening the couple attended an opera in the theatre of San Benedetto, which was converted into a dining hall the following day.[19] As one might expect, the celebrations, complete with regattas, bullfights, *Forze d'Ercole*, fireworks, operas, and theatrical spectacles, lasted for several days.[20]

Notes

1 See A. Giurgea, 'Theatre of the Flesh: The Carnival of Venice and the Theatre of the World', PhD diss., University of California (Los Angeles, 1987), pp. 55–80.

2 See P. Fortini Brown, *Venice and Antiquity,* (New Haven and London, 1996), especially 'A Noble Bloodline'.

3 D. Reato, *Storia del Carnevale di Venezia* (Venice,1991), p. 31–33.

4 For more information about Croce's *Mascarate*, see J. Gustafson Donnamae, 'Giovanni Croce's "Mascarate Piacevoli et Ridicolose per il Carnevale": A Contextual Study and Critical Edition', PhD diss., University of Minnesota (Minneapolis, 1992).

5 Ibid.

6 The most recent study of the *compagnie della calza* is, M. Casini, '*The compagnie della calza*: Pageantry, Politics and Courtly Manners in Renaissance Venice', *Center* 18, June 1997–May 1998, pp. 52–55. See also L. Venturi, *Le compagnie della calza (sec. XV-XVI)* (Venice, 1909).

7 P. Fortini Brown, *Narrative Painting in the Age of Carpaccio* (New Haven and London 1988), p. 240. Brown's study remains the best source for Carpaccio's narrative painting.

8 A. Giurgea, 1987. Giurgea's dissertation is the best study of the 'Theatres of the World'. In my analysis I retrace most of his fascinating theory. See also L. Zorzi, *Il Teatro e la Città. Saggi sulla Scena Italiana,* (Turin, 1977); L. Padoan, Urban, 'Gli spettacoli Urbani e l'utopia', *Architettura e Utopia nella Venezia del Cinquecento,* ed. L. Puppi (Milan, 1980), pp. 144–66.

9 A. Giurgea, 1987, p. 410–20.

10 Ibid.

11 See M. Tafuri, 1989, pp. 103–38.

12 On the phenomenon of triumphal entries in the Renaissance see B. Mitchell, *The Majesty of the State: Triumphal Progresses of Foreign Sovereigns in Renaissance Italy, 1494–1600* (Florence, 1986). Mitchell explains the dramatic climax of these entries as an 'emotional catharsis' invested with a peculiarly civic spirit.

13 A. Giurgea, 1987, pp. 57–58.

14 Ibid. pp. 65–68.

15 Ibid. p. 73.

16 In addition to Giurgea's interesting commentary, 1987; see the primary sources: M. Della Croce, *L'historia della pubblica et famosa Entrata in Vinegia del Serenissimo Henrico III re di Francia et Polonia* (Venice, 1574); P. Buccio, *Le coronationi di Polonia et di Francia del Christianissimo Re Henrico III* (Padua, 1576), pp. 177–79; P. De Nolhac and A. Solerti, *Il Viaggio in Italia di Enrico III Re di Francia e le Feste a Venezia, Ferrara, Mantova e Torino* (Turin, 1890), pp. 3–27.

17 See M. Rosenthal, *The Honest Courtesan* (Chicago and London, 1992).

18 A. Giurgea, 1987, pp. 165–80.

19 The custom of dining in a theatre became a Rococo obsession for aristocrats from all over Europe and especially in the Venetian Carnivals.

20 From the eighteenth century, theatre and 'Theatres of the World' assumed different aspects and meanings. Theatres were stages for comedies and tragedies while 'Theatres of the World' remained spectacular allegorical structures for receiving foreign dignitaries. See G. Bellorato Netanevi, *Breve descrizione di Venezia e de'piacevoli trattenimenti, che godea prima che s'introducessero i teatri, e che tutta via gode, in tutte le quattro stagioni dell'anno, ed in particolare in tempo di Carnovale* (Venice, 1715).

Rendezvous at Caffè Florian

Expressions of Carnivalesque
narcissism

Comedy and Curiosity

The artistically charged atmosphere of sixteenth-century Venice fostered the development of popular comedy.[1] Humanist intellectuals and poets of the calibre of Niccolò Machiavelli, Dovizi Bibbiena, Ludovico Ariosto, Pietro Aretino, Torquato Tasso, Ludovico Dolce, Ingegneri and Andrea Calmo experimented with comedy and organised numerous performances. Dolce, Calmo and Ingegneri worked very actively in Venice, Padua and Vicenza. Padua, with its important university and refined villas, had become a centre of study for ancient comedy. Vicenza, home of Palladio's Teatro Olimpico, came to be recognised as a great centre for theatrical production. In Venice the floating platforms remained the primary stages for humanist allegory, while the city's squares and newly built theatres became experimental venues for less esoteric and more popular drama.[2]

A new form of comedy appeared in Renaissance Venice alongside the older humanist theatrical tradition. The second half of the sixteenth century saw Giorgio Vasari designing a temporary theatre *all'antica* for the production of *La Talanta*, a comedy written by his contemporary Dovizi Bibbiena. Some years later Antonio Pigatta's *Antigono* was performed in a temporary theatre designed and built by Palladio. Pastoral, arcadian and classical themes were cleverly combined for the delectation of the *cognoscenti* who increasingly developed an interest for the action on stage. Almost simultaneously, some 'minor figures' such as Tommaso Mezzo and Giovanni Antonio Marsi contributed to the development of comedy in more modest venues and in public open spaces. Like their humanist predecessors they revived the ancient world of Plautus and Terentius, yet went much further, transforming the cold sterile theatre of the past into something much more lively with buffoons as actors. The latter, often wearing masks, were a huge success with the audiences and greatly aided the development of the comic genre.

In spite of the scorn heaped on them by intellectuals, the buffoons' success increased among the lower classes. Late Renaissance intellectuals such as Marcantonio Sebellico, Giovan Battista Seita, Paolo Canal and Girolamo Amaseo were in praise of the new dramas, but many believed the buffoons were corrupting the dignity of antiquity. Paradoxically, as Adrian Giurgea points out, the buffoons not only spread ancient culture among the lower classes, but were also great actors with an uncanny ability to parody the real world.[3] Zuan Polo, Domenico Taiacalze, Andrea Razer and Zuan Cimador were among the most famous masked actors of the Renaissance capable of acting while simultaneously impersonating

Aperitif at Caffè Florian

72

the character of the mask. The actor Cherea and the legendary Ruzzante developed a 'school' of comedy and mask that reached its zenith in Italy with the *commedia dell'arte* and abroad with the Comedie Francaise. Both the Italian and French comic styles depended upon the use of masks and the invention of hilarious characters.

It was the eighteenth-century Venetian playwright Carlo Goldoni who raised the *commedia dell'arte* to a new level of greatness. Goldoni argued that comedy had significant poetic content and went out of his way to defend the skill of its actors. He claimed that: '*la Commedia è poesia da rappresentarsi, e non è difetto suo che ella esiga, per riuscir perfettamente, de'bravi Comici che la rappresentino, animando le parole col buon garbo d'un'azione confacevole . . .*'[4] Goldoni's comedy was generally based on the relationship between servant and lord, a *concetto* with a long tradition. The Zanni (servants), also called Francatrippe, Arlecchino or Pulcinella, and the Magnifico (lord), often known as Pantalone, were the subjects for many of his comic sketches. Works such as *La locandiera, I rusteghi, La vedova scaltra, La bottega del caffè*, and especially *Arlecchino servitore di due padroni* and *Gli ultimi giorni di carnevale* were inspired by Carnival and exemplified its spirit with its jokes, paradoxes, comic use of dialects and role reversals.

These comedies led to the development of a wide variety of masks, fashioned for male and female caricatures. Comic protagonists such as Mirandolina, Corallina, Rosaura, Emilio Zago and Don Marzio, shared the stage with bizarre characters wearing masks: Arlecchino, Pulcinella, Colombina, Pantalone, Brighella and the Dottori. As the comedies became increasingly intricate they began to include sub-plots such as young men in search of their lovers. Lello, Flavio and Cinzio were stock names for handsome youths who, distracted and clumsy, were perpetually inflamed by love. Often a malevolent antagonist would stalk a victim, adding a twist to the plot. The most famous evil character was the powerful Capitan Spaventa, impersonated by actors who were able to frighten the audience.[5] Comic writers of the eighteenth century sought to create dramas of hilarious confusion based upon misunderstandings between masters and servants or between lovers; contrasting good and evil, innocence and corruption, beauty and hideousness.[6]

Surprisingly, the masks of the *commedia dell'arte* were rarely worn by Venetian citizens. Arlecchino, Pulcinella and Capitan Spaventa were theatrical personages for the stage and not the streets. They did not relate to the ordinary lives of Venetian citizens, who in reality

VENICE CARNIVAL

Contemple-les mon ame; Ils sont vraiment affreux!
Pareils aux mannequins, vaguement ridicules;
Terribles, singuliers comme les sonnanbules . . .

(Baudelaire, 'Les Aveugles')

were highly regulated by the state. The authorities constantly sought to limit the excessive opulence of the nobles' costumes, which tended to highlight the city's inherent social inequalities. Consequently, the mysterious-looking *bautta* and the more feminine *moretta* evolved in the eighteenth century and became the common masks of rich and poor alike.

The *bautta* was a simple mask with a large protruding beak that left the mouth partially exposed in order to facilitate breathing, speaking, eating and drinking. It was worn with a black mantle (*tabarro*) and a tricorn. Since the tricorn was attached to the *bautta* with strings it was never removed, not even to greet or dine. This mask, also known by the Latin *larva* (ghost or soul), gave its wearer a macabre, phantasmal aspect evoking that typically Carnivalesque rapport between the dead and the living. The nobles, recognised as such because they were usually accompanied by their *codeghe* (lantern-bearers), must have appeared quite spectral, if not frightening, when promenading down the narrow Venetian alleyways at night wearing a *bautta,* their shadow-like mantles flowing behind them.

The *bautta* was usually white and worn by men and women while the *moretta* was black and was an exclusively female object. The latter was a hypnotic round mask that covered the central part of the face (mouth, nose and eyes) but left the ears, forehead, chin and hair exposed. It was held in place not by strings or hairpins but by a bit held between the teeth. As a result its wearer could not speak, transforming the disguise into an enchanting seductive stratagem. Both the *bautta* and *moretta* were worn in accompaniment with a simple mantle which often concealed a sumptuous costume to be revealed only in the privacy of a palace. The effectiveness of Venetian masks in the 1700s therefore relied more on their suggestive allure than on luxurious materials and decorations.

Exhortation

With six months of Carnival each year the craft of mask-making evolved into a veritable art form, with thousands being produced every season. In 1400 the mask-makers (*mascareri*) organised themselves into a corporation and merged with the Painters Guild. By the eighteenth century there were at least twelve large workshops producing masks in the city centre.[7] Although the artists turned out numerous *bautte* and *morette* they also created less orthodox masks, many of which had a rather grotesque appearance. These had names like Mattaccino 'little crazy man', Wild Man, Bernardon, Doctor of the Plague and Tonin Bonagrazia.[8] The gradual relaxation of government regulation between the sixteenth and eighteenth centuries saw a notable shift towards wild libertine parties of masked revellers.

Conspiracy

Reinventing the past

Expressions of Venetian hedonism

Animals were used for cruel spectacles but after 1700 they were imported from Africa and the Orient to be exhibited publicly. Areas of eighteenth-century Venice were transformed into zoos packed with thousands of gaping spectators. The Rialto Bridge, the busiest point of the city, became a stage for bull races as attested by Gabriel Bella's painting in the Querini Stampalia. Riva degli Schiavoni, the long boardwalk south of Piazza San Marco, was crowded with *casotti* (cabanas) filled with animals from all over the world. A mysterious painting by Francesco Guardi depicts masked Venetians admiring a rhinoceros. Such animals were publicly displayed not only for mere show, but to celebrate the presence of Venetian merchants and ambassadors in distant lands. Bulls, horses and bears reminded the citizenry of the Republic's presence on the mainland, while rhinoceroses, giraffes, monkeys and elephants were evidence of Venetian activity in Asia and Africa. The Cicogna Codex[9] contains a description by an anonymous visitor to the Serenissima who saw camels, dromedaries, lions, tigers, panthers, horses, rhinoceros, wolves, monkeys and elephants. Some of the animals had been tamed and could respond to questions or solve mathematical riddles by moving various parts of their bodies. There was even a two-headed goat with six legs and four horns. The poet Pietro Buratti tells of an elephant that escaped from its cage and entered the church of Sant' Antonin where, with the permission of the patriarch, it was killed by the authorities.[10]

Deformed or disfigured humans were also exhibited: dwarfs, giants, strongmen, strongwomen and others. A sixteen-year-old French girl was curiously admired for her gigantic stature,[11] while a Flemish woman was applauded for pulling a horse with her hair.[12] A man could break an iron chain with his bare hands, while another could pull hundreds of kilos with his teeth. As evidenced in a cycle of paintings by Gian Domenico Tiepolo, executed in the late 1770s, Venetian urban spaces became the stages for charlatans, vendors, magicians and story tellers. The cycle, now in the Museo Correr, is part of an artistic tradition of *vedute* (panoramic views) of Venice in which fantastic architecture serves as a backdrop for bizarre characters and strange animals.

While always fascinated by the weird and the occult, in the Carnival season Venetians also paid homage to human intelligence and invention. Unusual machines were often objects of much curiosity. The *Mondo Novo* or 'New World' was a type of kaleidoscope through which Venetians could see images of distant lands, often distorted by reflecting

mirrors and perspectival manipulations. Such illusionistic devices parodied the real world, turning it upside down like Carnival itself. In the Baroque era, Swiss clockmakers surprised even the hardest cynics with moving dolls called *Droz*. These ingenious and extravagant creations increasingly stupefied and captivated both Venetian citizens and visitors alike as they gazed at the many 'cabinets of curiosities' assembled in Venice.

Afternoon chocolate at the Luna Baglioni Hotel

Notes

1 For more information about comedy and Carnival see A. Giurgea, 'Theatre of Flesh: The Carnival of Venice and the Theatre of the World', PhD diss., University of California (Los Angeles, 1987), pp. 230–80.

2 N. Mangini, *I teatri di Venezia* (Milan, 1974).

3 A. Giurgea, 1987, p. 256.

4 *Carlo Goldoni: dalle Maschere alla Commedia*, ed. C. Ferrari (Venice, 1957), p. 3. 'Comedy is performed poetry and it is not its fault that it requires, in order to turn out perfectly, good comedians to perform it, reciting the words with relevant actions.'

5 It is difficult to trace the origins of many of the comic characters and their masks. Generally, they seem to derive from the ancient *Atellane*, the mime spectacles performed in Magna Grecia. The *Atellane* mimes known as *Pappus*, *Maccus*, and *Dossenus* foreshadowed the characters of both Renaissance and eighteenth-century *commedia dell'arte*.

6 T. Holme, *A Servant of Many Masters: the Life and Time of Carlo Goldoni* (London, 1986).

7 D. Reato, 1991, pp. 43–44.

8 For more information about these masks, see V. Malamani, *La satira del costume a Venezia nel secolo XVIII* (Turin and Naples, 1886); G. Lorenzetti, *Le Feste e le Maschere Veneziane* (Venice, 1937); D. Reato and M. Obici, *Maschere e Travestimenti nella tradizione del Carnevale di Venezia* (Venice, 1981); *Il Carnevale Veneziano nelle Maschere incise da Francesco Bertelli*, ed. L. Padoan Urban (Milan, 1986).

9 Cod. Cicogna 2991–II, 68, Venice, Museo Correr, published in D. Reato, 1991, pp. 101–12.

10 *Poeta libertino*, ed. D. Reato (Venice, 1985).

11 Cod. Cicogna, 2991–II, 71, Venice, Museo Correr, published in, D. Reato, 1991, pp. 101–12.

12 Ibid.

Like the Western and Oriental kings
who met in the Lagoon at Mardi Gras
in Voltaire's *Candide*, contemporary
nobility continues the poetic tradition
of enjoying the cosmopolitan
atmosphere of the Carnival

Decadence and Transgression

In the midst of the crowds of masked revellers, animals and curious objects of all sorts, the eighteenth-century Serenissima slowly slipped into decadence. Although its military and economic might had long been on the wane, in the decades after 1700 Venice was still one of the biggest and richest capitals in Europe and as such drew great numbers of visitors. By that time most of its democratic ideals had all but dissipated as much of its wealth derived from corrupt practices. For example, nobles and pseudo-nobles paid huge bribes in order to appear in the Golden Book, (a list of members of the nobility), thereby replenishing the coffers of the city. The new revenues were then recycled into public entertainments and spectacles, attracting more visitors from abroad. In Voltaire's *Candide* the protagonist meets a series of sovereigns from both Christian Europe and the Orient; all had come to enjoy the general atmosphere of Carnival decadence. By the end of the eighteenth century the entire Lagoon had been transformed into a vast port of corruption, where people from all over the world met to gamble and enjoy sensuous and frivolous pleasures.

Vice

Interspersed throughout the city were gambling houses called *ridotti*, the forerunner of the modern casino. A well-known painting from Pietro Longhi's workshop exhibits a group of men, women and children in *bautte* and *morette* enjoying themselves in one of these casinos, apparently an elegant eighteenth-century foyer. It was in the hidden spaces behind the foyer, however, that the gambling actually took place. In quieter rooms visitors played at *bassetta*, *faraone*, *biribisso*, *panfil* and *sette e mezzo*.[1] The *ridotti* and their illicit activities eventually became so out of hand that in 1774 the Republic decreed that they must all be closed. Nevertheless, the law was not immediately and strictly enforced and gambling spread unabated into the *botteghe del caffè*, coffee houses furnished with secret gambling annexes that proved even more difficult to control.

The final years of the Republic saw criminal activity such as money laundering, prostitution and homicide become widespread. Corruption of every kind was rampant and infiltrated every corner of the city, even theatres and convents.[2] The narrow Venetian alleyways as well as gondolas and private palaces were places for betrayal, espionage, assassination and romantic encounters – heterosexual and homosexual.[3] Many eighteenth-century commentators were scandalised by masked prostitutes who met their clients in the brothels and streets.[4] Honest courtesans, who had delighted the nobles with love, poetry and physical pleasure only two centuries previously, were few and far between in the Settecento.

Now *Cicisbei* (gigolos) accompanied married ladies to meet their lovers in obscure streets, on gondolas, outside convents or in private palaces.[5] Homosexuality was commonplace. One of the most popular Venetian masks was the *gnaga*, a man dressed as a peasant woman with a mask recalling a cat. The *gnagas*, caricatures of vulgarity and sexual provocation, sought to imitate the spoken language of the lower classes with animalesque additions. The entire city had evolved into a world of licentiousness.

The numerous theatres of Venice were venues in Carnival season for spectacle and transgression. Giacomo Casanova reports that female and male prostitution spread in the lower-class seating section, which after the play became a kind of brothel foyer.[6] Paradoxically, the libertine Casanova suggests that the candles should not be extinguished until all spectators have exited! An engraving by Domenico Fossati for Walton Seriman's book *I Viaggi al Paese Delle Scimmie* shows the interior of a Venetian theatre during the second half of the eighteenth century. In this fascinating image a Rococo spectacle is attended by a masked audience of *bautte* who, half-distracted, enjoy the performance while talking mysteriously among themselves. It is a well-known fact that spectators in Venetian theatres could not keep silent during the performances and shouted comments at the actresses and *castrati*.

Promiscuity during Carnival pervaded convents and monasteries and nuns and friars participated in the lustful festivities. In his memoirs, Casanova recalls his sensuous encounter with a nun in an island monastery; these meetings appear to have been commonplace. A painting by Francesco Guardi at Cà Rezzonico scandalously depicts elegant men and women in the nuns' parlour of San Zaccaria. Moreover, Giorgio Baffo describes in explicitly erotic and at times pornographic terms the antics and perversions of the Venetians.[7]

Eventually the Council of Ten felt it necessary to create new legislation in order to prevent un-Christian activity in religious buildings.[8] They drew up new regulations called the *leggi delle pompe* in order to moderate pomposity during the festival and maintain a level of decorum.[9] Danilo Reato has published some of the prohibitions relating to the masquerade season, including the famous sumptuary laws that sought to banish excess from the city.[10] The laws aimed to reduce class disparity, danger in the streets, overly luxurious costumes and blasphemous language. Numerous rubrics calling for the elimination of private arms suggest the hazards of walking in certain quarters at night. From the thirteenth

85

century the Council of Ten had restricted nocturnal masquerades, while a law passed in the fifteenth century and constantly renewed prevented men disguised as women from entering convents. The Council's decrees during the Renaissance became more numerous and stringent. In a plague outbreak all public amusement was absolutely prohibited. Notwithstanding, a decree enacted in 1608 reveals that even in times of plague the festivities continued clandestinely.

Punishments for offenders were extremely severe. Men could be imprisoned for up to two years and condemned to serve as galley slaves for several months. Women, especially prostitutes, could be publicly whipped from Piazza San Marco to the Rialto Bridge, displayed as *meretrix* between the columns of the Piazzetta and exiled for four years. Both men and women were fined for ignoring the sumptuary laws regarding dress. Excessive gold, silver, stones, beads, lace and silk were forbidden, yet many patricians preferred to pay the penalties rather than dress down. When the Council obliged aristocratic women to wear black dresses in order to curb their rich and colourful costumes, lower-class women began to dress in black in order to resemble the richest ladies of the Grand Canal. In response to the legislation, the nobles instructed their tailors to create the most luxurious dark costumes possible.

Sumptuary laws reveal a paradox in Venetian society in the Carnival season. Eighteenth-century women were compelled to wear a mask upon entering a theatre and other public spaces: 'Women without a mask will not be allowed to enter the theatre' commanded a 1776 regulation.[11] The doorman of the San Luca, one of the city's seven main theatres, reported that when he asked the noblewoman Giulia Tron to disguise herself before entering the salon she replied with a pretentious insult: 'You are crazy!' and went and sat in her private *palco*.[12] As a result Giulia Tron was forced by magistrates to stay in her palace for at least three weeks. By obliging everybody to wear similar masks and costumes the Republic attempted to avoid disparity among classes and protect the dignity of important women. Oddly, masks became the uniform of a female society in which prostitutes, courtesans, nobles and citizens were, at least in the public domain, equally dressed. Lady Tron's refusal to wear a mask reveals the irony that in eighteenth-century Carnival, transgression and irreverence were actually expressed by not wearing a mask. Giulia Tron could not have imagined that only a few years later disguise would have been prohibited.

On the way to the grand ball

Notes

1 On gambling in Venice see G. Dolcetti, *Le Bische e il Giuoco d'Azzardo a Venezia* (Venice, 1903).

2 For delinquency in Renaissance and Settecento Venice see L. Menetto and G. Zennaro, *Storia del Malcostume a Venezia nei Secoli XVI e XVII* (Abano Terme, 1987).

3 *Agenti Segreti Veneziani nel '700*, ed. G. Comisso (Milan, 1941), p. 179.

4 Ibid. p. 191.

5 C. Lorenzoni, 'Cicisbei sul Liston', *La Lettura*, 24, n.10, 1924, pp. 797–98.

6 *Agenti Segreti Veneziani nel '700*, ed. G. Comisso (Milan, 1941), p. 179.

7 *Raccolta Generale delle Opere di Giorgio Baffo, Patrizio Veneto*, ed. E. Bartolini (Milan, 1971).

8 E. Volpi, *Storie intime di Venezia Repubblica* (Venice, 1893).

9 'Pompe' refers to exhibitionism and showing off. C. Ivanovich, *Minerva al tavolino . . . con Memorie teatrali di Venezia* (Venice, 1681), p. 37–81, writes about the opening of Carnival on the feast of St Stephen and remarks that 'le maschere fanno pompa di sè stesse' ('the masks show themselves off').

10 D. Reato, *Storia del Carnevale di Venezia* (Venice, 1991), pp. 86–89.

11 Ibid. p. 89. '*Alle dame sarà permesso l'entrare anche vestite con l'abito nero ch'é loro dalle leggi assegnato alle quali dame però, così vestite senza maschera non dovrà esser permesso l'entrar nella platea.*' (Ladies will be permitted to enter dressed also in black as decreed by law, but so-dressed without a mask, will not be permitted to enter the auditorium.)

12 Ibid. p. 89. The doorman of the theatre reported to the magistrates: '*Tosto da me avvertita di doversi poner in maschera, e per supremo comando, volle nullaostante entrare, col dirci siete pazzi. Da uno dei miei uomeni fu seguita sino al palco . . . e fule replicando lo stesso comando, ma essa N.D. serrò il palco, ne diede retta alcuna.*' (Having being warned, by supreme order, by myself, to wear a mask, [the lady] wanted all the same to enter, saying we were mad – she was followed by one of my men up to the box . . . and the same order was repeated to her, but she gripped the box and didn't pay any attention).

A scene reminiscent of a painting by Boucher

89

At night, while the palazzos of the
Grand Canal become temples of
hedonism and transgression, the
urban spaces around San Marco are
populated by haunting presences,
which transform the city into a surreal
space where silence and darkness are
suddenly broken by a swirl of lights
and the passage of a ghost

Strange phantoms rising as the mists arise
Dreadful, as hermit's dreams in haunted shades

(Alexander Pope, 'The Rape of the Lock')

Apex and Decline

The last two doges of Venice (Paolo Ranier and Ludovico Manin) witnessed the apex and decline of Carnival before its inexorable conclusion. In 1789 Doge Ranier, died but for a while Venetians were unaware of their ruler's death. The body was buried in secret in the church of the Tolentini without public ceremony for the Doge had died in the middle of Carnival, at a time when the state allowed burial but forbade mourning. For this reason, Ranier's death was made public only at Lent. When the patricians gathered in the Palazzo Ducale to elect the new doge they knew he would be the 118th doge of Venice but they never suspected he would be the last. About eight years after the election of Ludovico Manin, Napoleon's soldiers entered Piazza San Marco and declared the Serenissima their imperial territory. In May 1797, just before the beginning of the Ascension celebrations, which re-enacted the mystical marriage between Venice and the sea, Doge and patricians met for the last time in the Palazzo Ducale to declare the end of the Republic.

On the way to the ball

Doge Manin withdrew to his private apartments and symbolically gave over his ducal hat. 'There, having laid aside his ducal *corno*, he carefully untied the ribbons of the close-fitting cap of white linen worn beneath it, the *cuffietta*, and handed it to his valet, Bernardo Trevisan, with those sad words which, more than any others, seem to symbolise the fall of Venice: "*Tolè, questa no la adopero più*" (Take it, I shall not be needing it again).'[1] The counsellors, the procurators and the chancellors removed their symbolic black and red robes and escaped from the palace, frightened of the guillotine assembled in Piazza San Marco. Doge Manin must have mourned the death of the Republic seated underneath the canvases of Veronese, Tintoretto and Tiepolo, images that had represented for centuries the myth of *Venetia Figurata*: the city perceived as a beautiful woman, protected by the Virgin, identified with Venus, paralleled to Justice, superior to Rome, and venerated by all her citizens. The mask of Venice which, during the days of Carnival, extended to the entire Lagoon and symbolically to the cosmos, no longer had the talismanic magic power of the previous year. In July 1797, in a sad ritual, the Golden Book with the names of the noble members of the old oligarchic power was burned and the Venetian motto '*pax tibi Marce evangelista meus*' was replaced by the Napoleonic 'the rights of man and the citizens'.[2]

In the wake of the French invasion the law, now under foreign jurisdiction, became increasingly severe and Carnival almost disappeared. The subsequent Austrian dominion allowed masquerades only at private parties such as the Cavalchina at La Fenice, which became a kind of Hapsburg waltz ball. The French and Austrians prohibited the Carnival, yet its finale was a Venetian death. Once the Republic no longer existed and its sacred space had been violated, its citizens had no reason to rejoice the virginity and glory of their city. According to Danilo Reato, at this time Carnival was useless, for freedom, the foundation of joy, had vanished.[3] With the installation of a foreign governor it was not just Carnival that suffered: the subject of celebration, the myth of La Serenissima, lost its *raison d'être*.

A poem by Percy Shelley evokes the idea of a Venice no longer masked by pageantry but by death. The poet's words are infused with a romantic sentiment that subtly conveys the passage from the glorious past to contemporary gloom, from the myth of the Serenissima to the mask of death:

Shadows on the bridge

> Sun-girt City, thou hast been
>
> Ocean's child, and then his queen;
>
> Now is come a darker day,
>
> And thou soon must be his prey.
>
> The fisher on his watery way,
>
> Wandering at the close of day,
>
> Will spread his sail and seize his oar
>
> Till he pass the gloomy shore,
>
> Lest thy dead should, from their sleep
>
> Bursting o'er the starlight deep,
>
> Lead a rapid masque of death
>
> O'er the waters of his path.
>
> (Percy Bysshe Shelley, '*Lines Written Among the Euganean Hills*')

Notes

1 J. J. Norwich, *A History of Venice* (New York, 1989), p. 631.

2 A. Giurgea, 'Theatre of the Flesh: The Carnival of Venice and the Theatre of the World', PhD diss., University of California (Los Angeles, 1987). Giurgea's explanation of the end of the Carnival is a fascinating history of the decline of La Serenissima. For more information about Carnival in the last days of the Republic see H.L. Castonnet des Fosses, *Le carnaval de Venise au XVIII siecle. Les derniers Jours de la Republique* (Angers, 1866); and A. Pilot, 'Il Carnevale di Venezia nel 1847', *Gazzetta di Venezia*, 4 September, 1916. The article by Pilot witnesses the fact that after the French invasion and during the Austrian dominion the Venice Carnival did not fully die.

3 D.Reato, *Storia del Carnevale di Venezia* (Venice, 1991), p. 90. Venezia 'Non è più la città del Carnevale, è solo una piccola provincia dell' impero, che importano dunque le piccole concessioni, quando manca la libertà?'

Un'assidua discordia tra l'espressione delle labbra e quella degli occhi genera il mistero; par che un'anima duplice vi si riveli con diversa bellezza, lieta e triste, gelida e passionata, crudele e misericorde, umile e orgogliosa, ridente e irridente; e l'ambiguità suscita l'inquietudine nello spirito che si compiace delle cose oscure.

(Gabriele D'Annunzio, *Il Piacere*)

The Revival of Carnival

Under the French and Austrian dominions the Venice Carnival was reduced to a formal waltz ball within the private world of palaces and theatres until its suppression during the 1930s Fascist dictatorship. In 1980, almost two hundred years after Napoleon's invasion and around fifty years after Mussolini's regime, Carnival was resurrected with great fervour as a reaction to a period of terrorism that shocked Italy during the 1970s.

In the twentieth century the major Italian cities had no tangible reminders of the great triumphal Renaissance and Baroque Carnival processions. The ancient spectacular feasts of Rome, Florence and Naples, sponsored by popes and kings and organised by artists like Andrea Palladio and Gian Lorenzo Bernini, followed the same sad destiny as the Carnival in Napoleonic Venice. In the 1950s a Carnival prophet, Besteguy, launched a challenge arguing that if New York was becoming the financial capital of the world, Venice could aspire to the role of the capital of hedonism and debauchery.[1] In his idealism Besteguy transformed Palazzo Labia into a palace of 'A Thousand and One Nights' and organised a memorable banquet where nobles, industrialists, artists and stars danced before the frescoes of *Cleopatra* by Tiepolo. Besteguy's Bacchanalia shocked the conservative class with its transgression and irritated the Marxists with its luxury, so much so that in Venice popular opposition became a powerful force.

Despite social and jurisdictional prohibitions the mask remained an integral part of Italian theatre and folklore. In Milan and Rome, Florence and Venice the *commedia dell' arte* was extremely successful, while in Sardinia, Sicily, Puglia and the Alps anthropologists found uninterrupted February cults related to ancient and medieval celebrations. However, the revival of the Venice Carnival in 1980 was not the result of a contagious enthusiasm spreading from the renovated popularity of a variety of Carnivalesque celebrations. The Venice Carnival is different and, more significantly than all other festivals, transcends tradition, manifesting a modern social and political message.

During the 1970s Italy underwent a metamorphosis as it came to rank among the five most industrialised nations in the world while it was still politically undecided between Left and Right, Communism and Christian democracy, Russia and America. Such a critical transition, ushered in by the Cold War and espionage, led to tension in all regions. In fact, the whole peninsula was traumatised by organised terrorism: Piazza Fontana, Piazza della Loggia, Aldo Moro, Bologna Station and Italicus are among the squares, railway stations,

The sound of footsteps, the shadows of the past

trains and people victimised by bombings and assassinations. Blame for these aggressions fell to the Red Brigade (the revolutionary Left), the Fascists sects and, more often, on some unidentifiable mystery. Moreover, foreign terrorists chose Italy as a target for international incursions, bombing airports, embassies and tourist areas, sowing fear and anxiety. Venetians had already experienced the devastating flood of 1966 which, with the consequent exodus of citizens towards the mainland, exacerbated the legend of a desolate Venice sinking in polluted water. No wonder, therefore, that Italians identified the sorrow of the 1970s with lead, one of the heaviest metals, calling that critical decade, *anni di piombo*.

By the end of the *anni di piombo*, Venetians were reviving the February Shrove Week as compensation for the misery they had suffered and as a social rebellion in the style of a 1968 'happening'. Count Emile Targhetta D'Audiffret di Greoux, a protagonist of contemporary Carnival, asserts: 'You [h]ave to remember that Italy [had] just come through the very unhappy years of Red Brigade activity, of kidnappings, Italy under siege, with terrorist bombs in Rome, Milan, Bologna. Unhappy for too long, there was a joyous reaction.'[2] However, the revival of Carnival was not merely a reaction against alienation, like post-war *dolce vita* in Rome, but a young social movement instilled with the spirit of anarchy.

The 1970s in Europe and America was a time of protest against traditional institutions and a celebration of anarchy over official culture.[3] Everywhere dissent took the form of open-air gatherings and concerts in a continuous 'Summer of Love' atmosphere, moving from schools and universities to streets and squares.

The 'happenings' of Piazza San Marco assumed the character of a liberation ritual, where social frustration was counteracted by communal joy and artistic creativity. In tandem with this resurrection of Carnival, the late 1970s and early 1980s saw a proliferation of creativity in the arts, a revival of theatrical festivals, music and the so-called 'Made in Italy' label. This was the time when Roberto Capucci and Valentino in Rome and Florence, followed by Gianfranco Ferrè, Giorgio Armani and Gianni Versace in Milan, started exporting Italian fashion worldwide. Imagination was not the prerogative of a happy few however, Venetian *campi* and *calli* began to display the talents of individual people. Carnival was not just a joyful communal celebration but an original creative competition. In Venice, people newly discovered themselves as revellers, designers and actors in one of the most beautiful spectacles of the last *fin de siècle*.

February is a cold and foggy month in the northern Adriatic and in the 1970s only a few

Un éclair . . . puis la nuit! Fugitive beauté
Dont le regard ma fait soudainement renaître,
Ne te verrai-je plus que dans l'éternité?

(Baudelaire, 'A une passante')

97

people (lovers, artists and movie directors) were wintering in the Lagoon. Most of the hotels closed after Christmas. Burano, Murano, Torcello and other islands seemed more distant from Piazza San Marco than today, while the velvet beach of the Lido was still coloured with the melancholic images of *Death in Venice*. On the island of Burano, among colourful houses painted blue, red, yellow and green, a spark of Carnival appeared. The young Buranesi put on masks and began teasing each other in streets and canals, throwing flour and *coriandoli* (confetti) incognito. Adults joined in the game and soon the gaiety spread to the island of Murano and finally to Piazza San Marco. In the spirit of ancient Carnival a boat race, the *vogalonga*, was organised, linking islands and city in a wide circuit.

The Venetians celebrated their 1979 February festivities with even more effervescence. According to Bruno Tosi, the president of the Maria Callas Association: 'The inspiration seemed to come from young people, but it caught on immediately. You suddenly saw housewives going to the supermarket wearing odd hats and strange pieces of clothing they'd found in the attic.'[4] Shop owners decorated their windows with funny items while barmen offered wine and *frittole* cakes for a convivial and intimate celebration. A few expert artisans, such as the outstanding maestro Guerrino Giano Lovato of the atelier Al Mondonovo, experimented with paper, gesso, wood and leather, reinventing, through careful study, the traditional masks of Venice.[5] Enthusiasm entered every corner of the city and touched even the critics of the art Biennale.

On the occasion of the 1979 Biennale directed by Sisto della Palma, Palazzo Grassi hosted one of the most fascinating exhibitions in the Lagoon: 'Venezia e lo spazio scenico'[6] ('Venice and Scenic Space').[6] The show presented an analysis of Venetian theatre from the Middle Ages to the eighteenth century, from both a literary and scenographic point of view. The literary content was supervised by director Maurizio Scaparro and the architectural aspects by architect Paolo Portoghesi. A series of thoughtful studies shed light on Carnival's origins, its protagonists and its theatres. The exhibition continued in the following year when, in February 1980, the inventive Scaparro proposed extending it into the city theatres and organised a festival of *la commedia dell'arte*. All the theatres, usually closed at this time of year, responded with great verve. La Fenice, Goldoni, Malibran, Ridotto and Avogaria put together operas, operettas, comedies and Carnivalesque plays in which masks ruled as absolute protagonists. More rudimentary stages were assembled inside

An eighteenth-century dandy framed
by an elegantly stuccoed ceiling

Le sale si empivano rapidamente; le
danze incominciavano . . . le coppie
turbinando esalavano profumi.

(Gabriele D'Annunzio, *Il Piacere*)

Palazzo Grassi, i Magazzini del Sale, in the church of San Samuele, and at the Rialto Bridge, Campo Santo Stefano, the Accademia and finally Piazza San Marco. These venues became the focus for Utopian experiments throughout the day and night.

As if the numerous theatrical venues were not sufficient, a Theatre of the World was assembled at Punta della Dogana in the dramatic space where the Grand Canal meets the Basin of St Mark. Like its ancient predecessors the postmodern pavilion, designed by the contemporary architect Aldo Rossi, was raised on a barge in imitation of Renaissance prototypes. Inspired by Ludovico Rusconi, Andrea Palladio, Vincenzo Scamozzi and others, Rossi created an eclectic contemporary building full of suggestions of the past. The new *theatrum* had to symbolise memory; thus its creator interpreted form and function as a dialogue with the civilisations that shaped the city. Byzantine, Gothic, Islamic, Armenian and classical styles were all subtly combined in the theatre's materials, decorations and silhouette. The floating structure was composed of a polygonal base, crowned by a conical dome supporting a sphere. Inside, the backdrop featured an actual window with a view of the city so that the spectators in the *cavea*, inspired by the Anatomic Theatre of Padua, could admire the most ideal of all backdrops, Venice itself.[7] According to Adrian Giurgea: 'In 1980, for a short time, the improbable Utopia of the Venetian Carnival flickered ephemerally under the sign of the theatre, creating the magic illusion of a return to a spirituality denied by the modern world.'[8]

On the night of Shrove Tuesday 1980, Piazza San Marco became the scene of a Babylonian 'happening'. On the previous Monday, Scaparro and Portoghesi walking on the wet deserted pavements of Venice could not have imagined what was to happen the next day. The two organisers remember: 'We could hear the echo of our own footsteps and could not stop asking: are they going to come?'[9] Throughout the afternoon of Shrove Tuesday people in masks of all kinds with costumes, some made at the last minute and others of incredible elegance, walked hastily towards Piazza San Marco as if attracted by a magnet. Invaded by thousands of people, the Piazza appeared bigger than usual. Without warning the masses started running under the lights of the Basilica or into the darkness of the porticoes, dancing to classical music, hard rock and the incessant rhythms of drums. Organised musical groups, spontaneous orchestras, screams and voices resurrected the spirit of Carnival. Drug addicts, prostitutes, megalomaniacs, intellectuals, traditionalists, postmodern satyrs and bacchantes participated in a dance of liberation that led Venice and the world into a new historical era. Joy and freedom overpowered misery and control.

Following the 1980 experiment, Carnival continued its spontaneous and organised 'happenings' with art and culture. In 1981 the theme chosen by Scaparro was 'The Carnival of Reason': a conceptual comparison of logic and folly. Palazzo Grassi hosted 'The Travels of Italian Comedians in Eighteenth-Century Europe', an exhibition that illustrated the journeys of Venetian actors and playwrights to France and other countries. Again, the *commedia dell'arte* pervaded the atmosphere of museums, theatres and piazzas according to a long tradition. A sense of delirium continued to animate the crowds of the piazzas and the parties in the palaces. Here superwoman Fiorella Mancini organised extravagant banquets, intellectual debates and Bacchanalia among Turkish baths, Oriental perfumes and velvets by Fortuny. Her eclectic store in Campo Santo Stefano functioned as a general headquarters for revellers from all over the world.

105

Reflecting on the imminent end of Carnival

In 1982, Mayor Mario Rigo allowed maestro Scaparro to organise even more extravagant events, which amazed those who had the fortune to witness them. He cleverly decided to merge the cultures of Naples and Venice, the two traditional realms of Italian theatre, into one of the highest forms of cultural fusion ever achieved in modern Italy. In the theatres Carlo Goldoni was joined by the contemporary Neapolitan Eduardo de Filippo, one of the leading playwrights of recent history. Eduardo's comedies were performed in dialect with Neapolitan actors of outstanding bravura such as Pupella Magio and Carlo Giuffrè.

In urban spaces the spectacle was even more dramatic. Hundreds of white Pulcinellas (the mask of Naples) arrived by train to be met by hundreds of colourful Arlecchinos (the mask of the Serenissima). Streets between the railway station and the city centre were dominated by the white costumes of the Pulcinellas, mixing happily with the red, green, yellow and blue costumes of the Arlecchinos in Piazza San Marco. The fantastic costumes and eccentric masks danced in unison in the hours before Lent until, with an instinctive impulse, the throng screamed for the burning of Pantalon, the puppet-king of anarchic Carnival. While the king was consumed by fire, the bronze Moors on the clock tower and the bells of the mighty Campanile announced Lent. Venice had unified the diverse languages, cultures and spirits of northern and southern Italy into a spectacle of immense beauty.

In 1986 Nereo Laroni (the new mayor), Augusto Salvadari (assessor) and Bruno Tosi

Les soleils mouillés
De ces ciels brouillés
Pour mon esprit ont les charmes
Si mistérieux
De tes taîtres yeux
Brillant à travers leurs larmes.

(Baudelaire, 'L'invitation au voyage')

(cultural entrepreneur) decided to organise an extremely refined spectacle. The *commedia dell' arte*, opera, classical ballet and an exhibition on the painter Guiseppe Arcimboldo gave birth to an elegant and more composite 'happening'. For a series of nights the Grand Canal, Piazza, and Piazzetta San Marco were transformed into a bazaar of illusions inhabited by imaginative masks and illuminated by a dramatic combination of candles and lasers that moved among the Oriental domes to the sounds of Monteverdi, Gabrielli and Vivaldi. At sunset the Basilica was bathed in golden light, the Piazza was lit up by eight huge Murano chandeliers and the palaces of the Procuratie by hundreds of ghostly alabaster-like *bautte* installed on the windows. As darkness fell, a never-ending stream of Chinese shadows was projected on the Palazzo Ducale facade.

Night was greeted with an artificial rain of golden leaves that covered a more composite and serene crowd of marvellous masks and costumes created by Italian designers and artists from around the world. Rossana Molinatti had recreated the *Kiss* by Klimt in a monumental costume of immense suggestion and poetry. Nevio Bertollo, inspired by Ertè, created Art Deco parrots with green, yellow and red feathers. A French couple was awarded the first prize for their perfect re-creation of eighteenth-century Sicilian marionettes (*pupi*). A Neapolitan group, shimmering in gold costumes, evoked medieval heralds. Milanese designer Andrea Fachinato pretended to have the power to change the seasons. Ferrara Fiammetta arrived with her ambassadors from the galaxies. Massimiliano and Antonella from Lake Como awakened crowds with the sound of their drums, reminding revellers that life is only a blow. Nino Bolgan and Piero Tobio enchanted and animated the Piazza with Enigma and Arlecchino respectively. What a wonderful atmosphere pervaded that night in Piazza San Marco! Even nature chose to participate in this exuberant and colourful affair and sent forth whirling flurries of snowflakes.

To honour the Oriental ambassadors invited by the city council for the occasion, the 1986 Carnival was named 'Lights of Venice – Lights of the Orient'. As in its ancient past, Venice received Armenians, Hebrews, Albanians, Dalmatians, Greeks, Turks and representatives from the eastern Mediterranean and beyond including emissaries from India, China and Japan. Italian actress Valentina Cortese, presented actors, masks, buffoons, dancers, and musicians conjured an aura of elegance and welcomed the Oriental ambassadors, who had symbolically reached Venice on the routes of Marco Polo. The spectacle climaxed

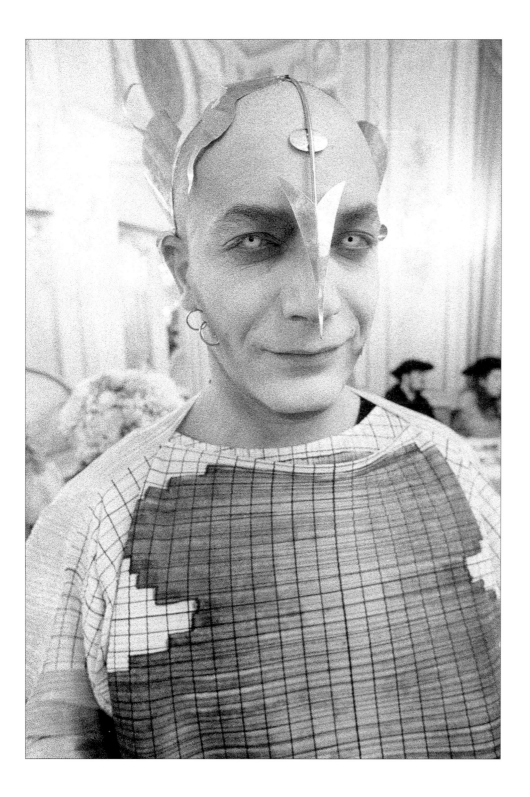

His face was deathly pale, and the lines of it were hard like drawn wires; the thick eyebrows that met over the nose now seemed like a heaving bar of white-hot metal.

(Bram Stoker, *Dracula*)

with the arrival of Giorgio Arvati, mask-maker *par excellence* of the newly reborn Carnival.

Arvati, architect, sculptor, painter and costume-designer of immense talent and technique, entered Piazza San Marco with his sister Annabella in the guise of 'Evil' and 'Good' respectively. Midway between an astral divinity and a classical warrior, Giorgio simultaneously represented the refined and macabre aspects of Venice Carnival. He focused all his energies and merged all his abilities, designing and realising the personifications of Good, an immaculately white angel, and Evil, a black phantasmal figure.

With dozens of metres of precious silk for the costume, hundreds of pieces of pure crystal for the masks, precious stones for the jewellery, and innumerable feathers for the wings, the two angels, black and white, hand in hand, shimmered among the lights of Piazza San Marco, complementing the beauty of the surroundings. 'The 1986 Carnival was so beautiful and magic that I levitated,' says Giorgio fifteen years later. He asserts that he frequents the Venice Carnival to 'perfect his megalomania' and to realise his dream, one day, of 'flying in front of the Basilica San Marco, like one of the Arsenal's angels, in order to gaze directly into the eyes of the bronze horses above the central portal'. His real spirit, however, is much less pretentious and more sensitive. Giorgio's aim is to fascinate children who, according to him, 'no longer have the possibility of experiencing fairy-tale beauty'. He currently persists in shocking the audiences, children and adults, of Piazza San Marco with monumental evocative creations: Nightmare, Zenith of the Sun, the Devil, Venetian Baroque, Roman Decadence, the Face Seller, the Guardian of Venice, the Husband of the Witch and the Allegory of the Swan.

The parade of black and white angels in Piazza San Marco coincided with the arrival of a floating theatre. A Theatre of the World supported by seahorses in a neoclassical style was carried through the Basin of Saint Mark in front of the Piazza. That night Carla Fracci, prima ballerina at La Scala in Milan, and the famous Nureyev, commenced a dance that ended with spectacular midnight fireworks. Lent began with the usual sound of the bells but the revellers of Piazza San Marco had seen a spectacle that had changed their lives.

The ingenuity of early 1980s Carnivals consisted not only of the originality of public events and the presence of incredible costumes, but also in the re-establishment of the ancient *compagnie della calza,* whose organisational skills contributed to extending pageants throughout the city. Some Venetians recreated *compagnie* called the Antichi,

The parallel between mask and
self is a typical Carnival game

directed by Prior Paolo Zane Cope, and the Nuovi Cortesi, supervised by Prior Carlo Ansaldo, for the purpose of generating coordinated transgression and acrobatic skill. The Antichi was undoubtedly the most irreverent among the groups. They directed the memorable Macabre Dance in Campo San Maurizio during the 'Carnival of Reason' with the purpose of giving tangible form to the irrational, if this is possible, by way of fantasy and magic.

Consciously or unconsciously, the Antichi propelled Bachtin's ideas into the modern world. In light of their success, the *compagnia* animated subsequent Carnivals with the Dance of Folly, the Dance of Love and Death, the Dance of the Courtesans and other mysterious rituals in a city that for a few weeks lived upside down in a Rabelaisian frenzy. The Cortesi were less transgressive and more in tune with the authorities. They, like similar Renaissance groups, tended to represent humanist culture and order. Through a long archival study the members of the Cortesi revived the ancient acrobatic spectacles: the *Forze d'Ercole*, the battles on the bridges and the dancing of the *moresca*.

Today, the Carnival atmosphere continues to live in the salons of the ancient palaces. Antonia Sautter's glorious 'Ballo del Doge' and Giovanna Barbiero's magnificent parties are by now traditional events that keep both the elegant and the grotesque aspects of Carnival alive. The two *anfitrione* of the Grand Canal welcome their masked guests, who arrive in decorated gondolas to the sound of violins. Under frescoes by Tiepolo or Guarana the beautiful Antonia and Giovanna, often guided by the eccentric Prince Maurice Agosti, prepare extravagant banquets where music and theatre amuse masked guests committed to their frivolous game of incognito.

The protagonist of the Venice Carnival is the city itself. Arriving in Venice in February is like entering a space between reality and vision: colours and shapes mirrored on the water, veiled by the fog, substances that conceal and enchant with the same authority as the mask. Venice was rediscovered as the ideal setting for the game of incognito.

What is happening to the inhabitants of the Lagoon? Ulderico Bernardi, Professor of Sociology at the University of Venice explains:

> Today's carnival is not just about group fashion but a re-emerging phenomenon decreed by individual questions, particularly among the youth of our postmodern society. Originally, the phenomenon was characterised by a periodic escape from a condition of mortification and reversal of values. Medieval Carnivals offered examples

Charme profond , magique, dont
nous grise Dans le present, le
passé restauré!

(Baudelaire, 'Le Parfum')

Iste ego sum . . . I burn with love of
my own self; I both kindle the
flames and suffer them . . .

(Ovid, *Metamorphoses*)

117

Pale spectres, gaping tombs, and purple fires:
Now lakes of liquid gold, Elysian scenes,
And crystal domes, and angels in machines.

(Alexander Pope, 'The Rape of the Lock')

of feasts of folly, feast of the donkey and the king child. Joking meant negation of hier-
archy, poverty was challenged with gluttony, dances and songs foreshadowed sexual
transgression. Today this spirit no longer makes sense. Modern Carnival is a social and
cultural protest. It is not a problem of flesh but of soul . . . Indeed, behind their masks,
young people aim at emphasising the uniqueness of their personalities.[10]

Undoubtedly, the modern Venice Carnival is a great device for the study of psychology and
sociology, especially with regard to issues relating to individual expression and peer pres-
sure. Men and women in mask are reflections of modern social issues concerning sexuality,
repression, freedom, exhibitionism, narcissism and, above all, the human desire to evoke
the past, to escape from reality and to explore a different identity.

The libertine pleasure of the
Venetian Carnival

120

The Venice Carnival has changed significantly in the course of its long history. Between
the Renaissance and Enlightenment Carnival represented aspects of politics, culture and
social behaviour: from an aristocratic exhibition of individual wealth and power to an
increasingly homogeneous masquerade that concealed the gap between patricians and citizens; from a rigidly controlled state spectacle in praise of the city's apotheosis to a libertine
festival in the wake of the city's decadence; from a humanist allegory to a laboratory of the
commedia dell'arte. Carnival, with theatrical exploration and urban spectacle at its core, was
the language of a city that perceived herself as a *bellissima donna*, imbued with the purity of
the Virgin, the beauty of Venus, the power of Dea Roma and the morality of Justice. When
Napoleon's troops invaded the Serenissima that *bellissima donna* was violated and deprived
of her mythical costume. The city's ephemeral form of communication, Carnival, no longer
made sense, for the traditional principles, peace and liberty, had vanished forever. With the
crises of the French and Austrian occupations, the suppression of the Fascist regime and,
more recently, the terrorist attacks during the *anni di piombo*, Venice had little to rejoice for
a long time, at least until 1980, when Carnival was reborn as a Woodstock-style 'happening'.
In the present millennium Carnival is more a fair of illusions than a spontaneous gathering.
Today the Lagoon is a place where people are spectators in an all-inclusive tourist package,
or masked protagonists in search of an escape from reality. Yet the Venice Carnival, glorious
and decadent, has once again become an esoteric means of communicating social reality,
unfolding as allegory in the most beautiful theatre in the world.

Watteau, ce carnaval où bien des coeurs illustre,
Comme des papillons, errent en flamboyant,
Décors frais et légers éclairés par des lustres
Qui versent la folie a ce bal tournoyant; . . .

(Baudelaire, 'Les Phares')

An acrobatic display stupefies a
beautiful guest at the Ballo del Doge

Notes

1 N. Salvalaggio, *Nostalgia dei Carnevali Perduti*, ed. A. Savella and G. Granzotto (Milan, 1984), p. 23.

2 P. Martin, 'Venetian Blinder', *The Sunday Times Magazine*, 11 July 1999, p. 42. Count Targhetta is one of the most interesting figures of contemporary Carnival. This sophisticated aristocrat, half-French half-Italian, is a man of indefinite age, a point of reference for the numerous French colonists who every February arrive in Venice to celebrate Carnival. The new French invasion is peaceful and elegant and brings a touch of Versailles to the Lagoon.

3 Anarchic protests coincided with the publication in Italy of Michail Bachtin's *Rabelais and His World*, which had a great impact on Italian intellectuals for its anarchic spirit. The famous book was published in Italian with the title *L'opera di Rabelais e la cultura popolare. Riso, carnevale e festa nella tradizione medievale e rinascimentale* (Turin, 1979). In the same decade Federico Fellini directed his own *Satyricon* and *Casanova*, Pier Paolo Pasolini filmed *Decameron* and *A Thousand and One Nights* and books and movies explored the grotesque, the enchanting and the masquerade as if these were congenial themes of postmodern society.

4 P. Martin, 1999, p. 41.

5 Lovato has been one of the main protagonists of the Carnival resurrection. He is a cultivated and talented artist who, through meticulous study, hard work and immense passion has revived the atmosphere of ancient Carnival in contemporary Venice, animating Piazza San Marco and other urban spaces with a peculiar Bachtian spirit. His masks reproduce sexual organs, excrement and grotesque figures impersonated by actors who have revived the blasphemous language of Carnival. Lovato's atelier 'Al Mondonovo' in Campo Santa Margherita should be regarded today as one of the relics of a Carnival which is, unfortunately, disappearing again.

6 *Venezia e lo spazio scenico*, exhibition catalogue, ed. M. Brusatin (Venice, 1979).

7 Rossi's fantastic and ambitious monument went to the city of Dubrovnik on a tour of former Venetian colonies. In August 1980 the Theatre of the World was transported by a motor boat along the Dalmatian Coast accompanied by the actors of the 'Avogaria'. From town to town the company played the comedy of the Zanni in the same way as that of previous centuries. This incredible event continued the spirit of the newly reborn Carnival throughout the summer and established links with cities and villages which had enjoyed, in the past, the glory of La Serenissima. At Carnival, on more than one occasion, Venice opened a cultural path with the states of former Yugoslavia, for both had shared a common history for many centuries. Hopefully Venice will re-appropriate this role of cultural bridge between Eastern and Western Europe in the immediate future. Carnival has been and could be an important instrument of communication, a festival where ideals of freedom, culture and peace are conveyed to the world.

8 A. Giurgea, 'Theatre of the Flesh: The Carnival of Venice and the Theatre of the World', PhD diss., University of California (Los Angeles, 1987), p. 652.

9 S. Nesi, 'La fiera dell'illusione', *Meridiani. Venezia*, I, 1, 1988, p. 33. Author's translation from: '*Dietro di noi sentivamo l'eco dei nostri passi e non potevamo fare a meno di chiederci: verranno?*'

10 D. Zamburlin, 'Cadono i tabù, sopravvive la libertà', *Guida al Carnevale di Venezia: luci di Venezia luci d'Oriente* (Venice, 1986), pp. 74–75.

At night in the urban labyrinth of Venice

Votre âme est un paysage choisi
Que vont charmant masques et bergamasques,
Jouant du luth, et dansant, et quasi
Tristes sous leurs deguisements fantasques.

(Verlaine, 'Clair de Lune')

THE REVIVAL OF CARNIVAL

VENICE CARNIVAL

Beyond suggestion . . . the alluring
power of a gaze, a gesture, a surreal
moment in a Venetian palazzo

Glossary

all'antica	antique style
bautta	mask with beak worn by men
botteghe del caffè	coffee houses
calli	main alleyway
calza	coloured hose
campi	squares
castrati	eunuchs
cavacani	dog trainers
cavea	auditorium
cicisbeo	married woman's gallant, gigolo
codega	lantern bearer
commedia dell'arte	16th-18th C, Italian popular comedy
Compagnie della Calza	carnival association
coriandoli	confetti
fabri	the ironworkers' guild
fabulae	allegorical celebrations
Forze d'Ercole	acrobatic displays
frittole	carnival cakes
gnaga	man dressed as a peasant woman
La Sensa	Feast of Ascension
Liston	parade of nobles in costume
Mardi Gras (French)	Shrove Tuesday
Martedì Grasso (Italian)	Shrove Tuesday
mascarate	aristocratic satires
mascareri	mask makers
moresca	a dagger dance
moretta	black mask worn by women
mumarie	allegorical celebrations
palco	theatre box/stage
pupi	Sicilian marionettes
quodlibet	carnival dance
ridotti	gambling houses
scenae	scenography
sestrieri	the six districts of Venice
settimana grassa	Shrove Week
tabarro	black mantle
Theatrum Mundi	Theatre of the World
tiratori	volunteers who hold a bull
villotta	carnival dance
vogalonga	Venetian boat race

In the swirl of a dance . . .

Concert at Palazzo Pisani Moretta

Le teste ingemmate si curvavano o
si ergevano; certe bocche
semiaperte brillavano come la
porpora; certe spalle nude
luccicavano sparse d'un velo
d'umidore; certi seni parevano
irrompere dal busto, sotto la
veemenza dell'ansia.

(Gabriele D'Annunzio, *Il Piacere*)

132

. . . My soul, from our first meeting,
burned with fires it had never
before known; but the fires were
not of Eros, and bitter and
tormenting to my spirit was the
gradual conviction that I could in
no manner define their unusual
meaning, or regulate their vague
intensity. Yet we met . . .

(Edgar Allan Poe, *Morella*)

Oh! Just, subtle, and mighty opium!
That to the hearts of poor and rich
alike, for the wounds that will never
heal, and for the pangs that tempt
the spirit to rebel, bringest an
assuaging balm; eloquent opium!

(Thomas de Quincey, *Confessions
of an English Opium Eater*)

Casanova seducing a lady

Thou only givest these gifts to man;
and thou hast the keys to Paradise,
oh, just, subtle, and mighty opium!

(Thomas de Quincey, *Confessions
of an English Opium Eater*)

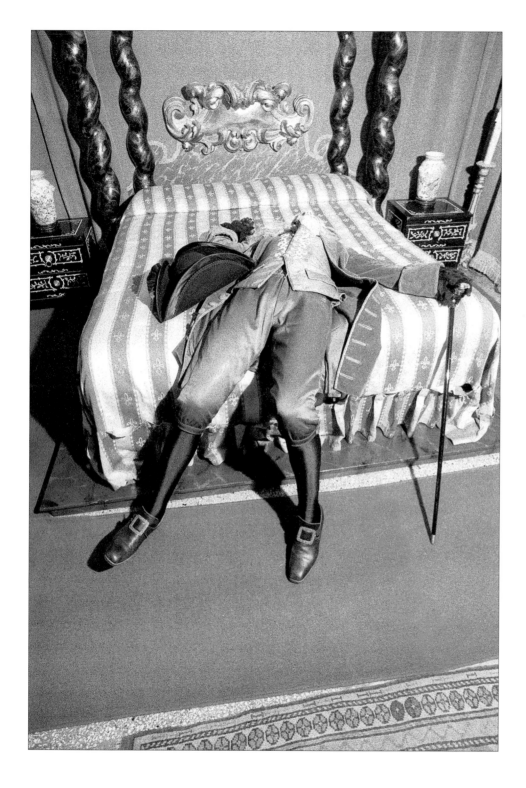

The bells of San Marco announce
Lent . . . Carnival is over . . . it is
time for the restitution of the self

. . . In Venice Tasso's echoes are no more,
And silent rows the songless gondolier;
Her palaces are crumbling to the shore,
And music meets not always now the ear:
Those days are gone but Beauty still is here.
States fall, arts fade but nature doth no die,
Nor yet forget how Venice once was dear,
The pleasant place of all festivity,
The revel of the earth, the masque of Italy.

(Lord Byron, *Child Harold*)